Backbone.js Cookbook

Over 80 recipes for creating outstanding web applications with Backbone.js, leveraging MVC, and REST architecture principles

Vadim Mirgorod

[PACKT] open source *
PUBLISHING   community experience distilled

BIRMINGHAM - MUMBAI

Backbone.js Cookbook

First published: August 2013

Production Reference: 1200813

Published by Packt Publishing Ltd.
Livery Place
35 Livery Street
Birmingham B3 2PB, UK.

ISBN 978-1-78216-272-8

www.packtpub.com

Cover Image by J.Blaminsky (milak6@wp.pl)

Credits

Author

Vadim Mirgorod

Reviewers

Ivano Malavolta

Jan Carlo Viray

Stephen Sawchuk

Acquisition Editor

Mary Nadar

Lead Technical Editor

Dayan Hyames

Technical Editors

Aparna Chand

Dylan Fernandes

Kapil Hemnani

Virgin Juanita

Project Coordinator

Kranti Berde

Copy Editors

Mradula Hegde

Insiya Morbiwala

Alfida Paiva

Adithi Shetty

Proofreader

Clyde Jenkins

Indexer

Hemangini Bari

Graphics

Abhinash Sahu

Production Coordinator

Manu Joseph

Cover Work

Manu Joseph

About the Author

Vadim Mirgorod is a professional web developer and an open source expert, who is passionate about technologies and innovations. He provides the code for the content management system Drupal and maintains several Backbone.js plugins. He is an active community member, who organized IT events in his city and spoke at the international conferences in Chicago, Munich, and Portland. His recent session at DrupalCon Portland was about Backbone.js.

The following are some of the highlights of his career:

- Presently he is running a company known as CoderBlvd (`http://www.coderblvd.com`), which is based in Ukraine. CoderBlvd provides IT outsourcing services for international businesses.

- (August 2010- August 2013)He worked in Trellon, LLC as a Lead Developer, creating CRM-based systems and web applications, using Drupal and PHP.

- (July 2009- August 2010)He used to give web development classes, when he was working in Donetsk National Technical University.

You can reach him through his website at `http://www.vmirgorod.name` or by connecting to his Twitter account `@dealancer`.

Acknowledgement

I would like to thank Mary Nadar, Anish Ramchandani, Kranti Berde, and Dayan Hyames at Packt Publishing for providing me an opportunity to write my first book and for their guidance, patience, and encouragement.

Also, I appreciate an incredible help from the review team in the person of Jan Carlo Viray and Ivano Malavolta, who provided their expertise to make this book more valuable.

Many thanks to all the people at the Backbone.js community, who provided me with immediate answers for all my questions. Also thanks to all the guys at `mongolab.com` for their service.

A huge thanks to Michael Haggerty, CEO of Trellon, for allowing me to take long hours off to complete this book and also for taking a look at some of the chapters.

And finally, I send all my love and thanks to my wife Julia and my son Artem for their immense support, patience, and faith in me.

About the Reviewers

Ivano Malavolta is a research fellow at the Information Engineering, Computer Science, and Mathematics department of the University of L'Aquila. He holds a Ph.D. degree and is currently doing research on mobile (web) apps development, software architecture, and model-driven engineering.

He is also teaching these topics in dedicated courses at the University of L'Aquila, for both bachelor and master degrees.

For what concerns his research activities, he is actively collaborating with the following institutions:

- Computer Communications Department (Middlesex University, London, U.K.)
- Software Engineering Group (VU University, Amsterdam, the Netherlands)
- Software Engineering Research Group (Istituto di Scienza e Tecnologie dell'Informazione A. Faedo ISTI - CNR, Pisa, Italy)
- School of Innovation, Design, and Engineering (Mälardalen University, Västerås, Sweden)

His main professional activities are listed as follows:

- (from December 2011) Freelance: Design and development of mobile and web applications.
- (May–February 2010) Software Architect & Project Manager, Tribe ICT business sector: Geographic Information Systems. His main responsibilities were design, management, and technological support for the development of a distributed, extensible, and customizable GIS framework. The system is based on the uDig platform (http://www.udig.org) and exploits the following technologies: Java, Eclipse (RCP, EMF, JFace), JTS, Geoserver, and Geonetwork.

- ▶ (October–February 2008) Developer, Medea ICT business sector: Information Technologies, document management systems. His main responsibilities were development of a document management system in accordance with Italian security laws for the Regione Abruzzo. The system has been implemented as a J2EE web application using the following technologies: Java, JSF, IBM DB2, Eclipse, Jboss, Hibernate, Acegi Security, and Ja-sig CAS single sign-on system.

Jan Carlo Viray is an aspiring entrepreneur with a background in business and web development. He has experience in .NET, PHP, Node.js, and is specializing in frontend development. He has a strong passion for growth and to help others reach their potential. He attributes all his talents and successes to God as he lives his life to the fullest daily. Making Jesus Lord of his life, he strives daily to be a *man of God*. He is a graduate of Cal State Long Beach, earning a title of *cum laude*. Nothing is impossible for him, because God is always by his side. He currently lives with his wonderful and loving wife at Los Angeles, CA. You can reach him through his website at www.jancarloviray.com or by connecting to his Twitter account @jancarloviray.

I would like to first and foremost thank God who has given me talents, opportunities, friendships, and blessings that has helped me throughout my life. I would also like to thank my parents, who have sacrificed so much to raise me and to help me have a great future. Lastly, I would like to thank my wife who has been very patient, respectful, loving, kind, and supportive in every way so that I can fulfill my dreams and live my life to the fullest.

www.PacktPub.com

Support files, eBooks, discount offers and more

You might want to visit `www.PacktPub.com` for support files and downloads related to your book.

Did you know that Packt offers eBook versions of every book published, with PDF and ePub files available? You can upgrade to the eBook version at `www.PacktPub.com` and as a print book customer, you are entitled to a discount on the eBook copy. Get in touch with us at `service@packtpub.com` for more details.

At `www.PacktPub.com`, you can also read a collection of free technical articles, sign up for a range of free newsletters and receive exclusive discounts and offers on Packt books and eBooks.

`http://PacktLib.PacktPub.com`

Do you need instant solutions to your IT questions? PacktLib is Packt's online digital book library. Here, you can access, read and search across Packt's entire library of books.

Why Subscribe?

- ► Fully searchable across every book published by Packt
- ► Copy and paste, print and bookmark content
- ► On demand and accessible via web browser

Free Access for Packt account holders

If you have an account with Packt at `www.PacktPub.com`, you can use this to access PacktLib today and view nine entirely free books. Simply use your login credentials for immediate access.

Table of Contents

Preface

Welcome to the *Backbone.js Cookbook*. We will learn how to create outstanding web applications using lightweight JavaScript framework known as `Backbone.js` and utilizing the superior rendering power of modern browsers.

Backbone.js Cookbook contains a series of recipes that provide practical, step-by-step solutions to the problems that may occur during the frontend application development, using an MVC pattern and a REST-style communication. You will learn how to build Backbone applications by utilizing the power of popular Backbone extensions and how to integrate your app with different third-party libraries. You will also learn how to fulfill the requirements of the most challenging tasks.

What this book covers

Chapter 1, Understanding Backbone, introduces you to an MVC pattern and `Backbone.js` framework. You will learn how to design Backbone applications in terms of MVC and will be able to create your first Backbone app using models, views, and routers.

Chapter 2, Models, helps you learn about `Backbone.Model`, the main building block of your application, which stores data and provides business logic.

Chapter 3, Collections, teaches you how to organize models in manageable sets known as collections, which allow you to perform different methods, such as sorting, filtering, iterating, and so on.

Chapter 4, Views, helps you learn how to use Backbone views to render models and collections, and how to intercept DOM events.

Chapter 5, Events and Bindings, tells you about event system used in `Backbone.js` and demonstrates event binding techniques.

Chapter 6, Templates and UX sugar, is devoted to the frontend enhancements that makes Backbone application look better and program easily.

Chapter 7, REST and Storage, is focused on how `Backbone.js` synchronizes models and collections with a RESTful backend or stores them in the HTML5 local storage.

Chapter 8, Special Techniques, helps you learn how to solve the most challenging problems that can occur during Backbone development, such as creating extensions, testing your app, creating a mobile app, and performing search-engine compatibility.

What you need for this book

Most of the recipes in this book do not require special software to be used. What you need is a browser and a text editor or IDE to edit HTML, JavaScript, and CSS files. Some of the recipes in *Chapter 7, Rest and Storage* and *Chapter 8, Special Techniques* require you to install GIT, Node.js, and NPM. It also assumes that you can use a Unix-like shell.

Who this book is for

This book is created for frontend developers who are familiar with JavaScript, HTML, and CSS. It assumes that you have good understanding of Object Oriented Programming (OOP) and some practice with the jQuery library.

Conventions

In this book, you will find a number of styles of text that distinguish between different kinds of information. Here are some examples of these styles, and an explanation of their meaning.

Code words in text, database table names, folder names, filenames, file extensions, pathnames, dummy URLs, user input, and Twitter handles are shown as follows: "To check if model has an attribute use the `has()` method. It returns `true` if the attribute exists, otherwise `false`."

A block of code is set as follows:

```
if (!invoiceItemModel.has('quantity'))
  {
    console.log('Quantity attribute does not exists!')
  }
```

When we wish to draw your attention to a particular part of a code block, the relevant lines or items are set in bold:

```
var InvoiceItemModel = Backbone.Model.extend
  ({
    // Define validation criteria.
    validate: function(attrs) {
      if (attrs.quantity <= 0) {
        return "quantity can't be negative or equal to zero";
      }
    }
  });
```

Any command-line input or output is written as follows:

```
$ npm install -g requirejs
```

New terms and **important words** are shown in bold. Words that you see on the screen, in menus, or dialog boxes for example, appear in the text like this: "When user clicks on the **Add** button, the following popup is generated and shown to the user:".

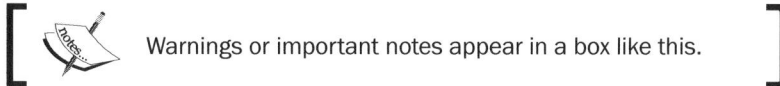

> Warnings or important notes appear in a box like this.

> Tips and tricks appear like this.

Reader feedback

Feedback from our readers is always welcome. Let us know what you think about this book—what you liked or may have disliked. Reader feedback is important for us to develop titles that you really get the most out of.

To send us general feedback, simply send an e-mail to feedback@packtpub.com, and mention the book title via the subject of your message.

If there is a topic that you have expertise in and you are interested in either writing or contributing to a book, see our author guide on www.packtpub.com/authors.

Customer support

Now that you are the proud owner of a Packt book, we have a number of things to help you to get the most from your purchase.

Downloading the example code

You can download the example code files for all Packt books you have purchased from your account at `http://www.packtpub.com`. If you purchased this book elsewhere, you can visit `http://www.packtpub.com/support` and register to have the files e-mailed directly to you.

Errata

Although we have taken every care to ensure the accuracy of our content, mistakes do happen. If you find a mistake in one of our books—maybe a mistake in the text or the code—we would be grateful if you would report this to us. By doing so, you can save other readers from frustration and help us improve subsequent versions of this book. If you find any errata, please report them by visiting `http://www.packtpub.com/submit-errata`, selecting your book, clicking on the **errata submission form** link, and entering the details of your errata. Once your errata are verified, your submission will be accepted and the errata will be uploaded on our website, or added to any list of existing errata, under the Errata section of that title. Any existing errata can be viewed by selecting your title from `http://www.packtpub.com/support`.

Piracy

Piracy of copyright material on the Internet is an ongoing problem across all media. At Packt, we take the protection of our copyright and licenses very seriously. If you come across any illegal copies of our works, in any form, on the Internet, please provide us with the location address or website name immediately so that we can pursue a remedy.

Please contact us at `copyright@packtpub.com` with a link to the suspected pirated material.

We appreciate your help in protecting our authors, and our ability to bring you valuable content.

Questions

You can contact us at `questions@packtpub.com` if you are having a problem with any aspect of the book, and we will do our best to address it.

1
Understanding Backbone

In this chapter, we will cover the following points:

- ▸ Designing an application with the MVC pattern
- ▸ Defining business logic with models and collections
- ▸ Modeling an application's behavior with views and a router
- ▸ Creating an application structure from scratch
- ▸ Writing your first Backbone application
- ▸ Implementing URL routing in your application
- ▸ Extending an application with plugins
- ▸ Contributing to the Backbone project

Introduction

Backbone.js is a lightweight JavaScript framework that is based on the Model-View-Controller (MVC) pattern and allows developers to create single-page web applications. With Backbone, it is possible to update a web page quickly using the REST approach with a minimal amount of data transferred between a client and a server.

Backbone.js is becoming more popular day by day and is being used on a large scale for web applications and IT startups; some of them are as follows:

- ▶ Groupon Now!: The team decided that their first product would be AJAX-heavy but should still be linkable and shareable. Though they were completely new to Backbone, they found that its learning curve was incredibly quick, so they were able to deliver the working product in just two weeks.

- ▶ Foursquare: This used the Backbone.js library to create model classes for the entities in foursquare (for example, venues, check-ins, and users). They found that Backbone's model classes provide a simple and light-weight mechanism to capture an object's data and state, complete with the semantics of a classical inheritance.

- ▶ LinkedIn mobile: This used Backbone.js to create its next-generation HTML5 mobile web app. Backbone made it easy to keep the app modular, organized, and extensible, so it was possible to program the complexities of LinkedIn's user experience. Moreover, they are using the same code base in their mobile applications for iOS and Android platforms.

- ▶ WordPress.com: This is a SaaS version of Wordpress and uses Backbone.js models, collections, and views in its notification system, and is integrating Backbone.js into the Stats tab and into other features throughout the home page.

- ▶ Airbnb: This is a community marketplace for users to list, discover, and book unique spaces around the world. Its development team has used Backbone in many latest products. Recently, they rebuilt a mobile website with Backbone.js and Node.js tied together with a library named Rendr.

You can visit the following links to get acquainted with other usage examples of Backbone.js:

```
http://backbonejs.org/#examples
```

Backbone.js was started by Jeremy Ashkenas from DocumentCloud in 2010 and is now being used and improved by lots of developers all over the world using Git, the distributed version control system.

In this chapter, we are going to provide some practical examples of how to use Backbone.js, and we will structure a design for a program named Billing Application by following the MVC and Backbone pattern. We will also refer to this structure in the later chapters of this book. Reading this chapter is especially useful if you are new to developing with Backbone.js. If you feel that you're an experienced developer, you can skip this chapter.

Designing an application with the MVC pattern

MVC is a design pattern that is widely used in user-facing software, such as web applications. It is intended for splitting data and representing it in a way that makes it convenient for user interaction. To understand what it does, understand the following:

▶ Model: This contains data and provides business logic used to run the application

▶ View: This presents the model to the user

▶ Controller: This reacts to user input by updating the model and the view

There could be some differences in the MVC implementation, but in general it conforms to the following scheme:

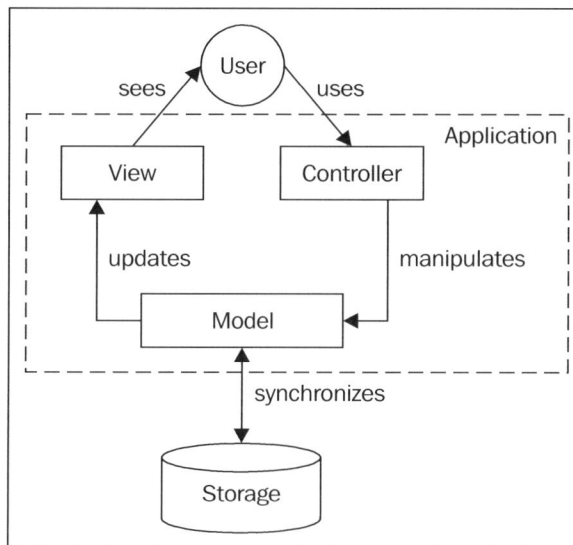

Worldwide practice shows that the use of the MVC pattern provides various benefits to the developer:

▶ Following the separation of the concerned paradigm, which splits an application into independent parts, it is easier to modify or replace

▶ It achieves code reusability by rendering a model in different views without the need to implement model functionality in each view

▶ It requires less training and has a quicker startup time for the new developers within an organization

To have a better understanding of the MVC pattern, we are going to design a Billing Application. We will refer to this design throughout the book when we are learning specific topics.

Our Billing Application will allow users to generate invoices, manage them, and send them to clients. According to the worldwide practice, the invoice should contain a reference number, date, information about the buyer and seller, bank account details, a list of provided products or services, and an invoice sum. Let's have a look at the following screenshot to understand how an invoice appears:

North American Veeblefetzer	INVOICE
	May 1, 2012
	Ref # INV1234

Beneficiary	North American Veeblefetzer 185 West 74th Street New York, New York United States Phone: 1-234-567-8912
Beneficiary Account	2000 4638 1116 1420
Bank	Bank of Columbus 320 Fowler Street Lynbrook, New York United States
SWIFT	BNCLMB11
Special Instructions	

Bill To: **Comments:**

John Smith
712 Red Bark Lane
Henderson, Clark County
Nevada 89011
United States
Phone: 1-987-654-3210

Products or Services:

Date	Description	Quantity	Unit Price	Amount
24 April, 2013	Wooden Toy House	3	22	66
24 April, 2013	Farm Animal Set	1	17	17

AMOUNT DUE
$83

How to do it...

Let's follow the ensuing steps to design an MVC structure for the Billing Application:

1. Let's write down a list of functional requirements for this application. We assume that the end user may want to be able to do the following:

   □ Generate an invoice

   □ E-mail the invoice to the buyer

   □ Print the invoice

   □ See a list of existing invoices

   □ Manage invoices (create, read, update, and delete)

   □ Update an invoice status (draft, issued, paid, and canceled)

   □ View a yearly income graph and other reports

2. To simplify the process of creating multiple invoices, the user may want to manage information about buyers and his personal details in the specific part of the application before he/she creates an invoice. So, our application should provide additional functionalities to the end user, such as the following:

   □ The ability to see a list of buyers and use it when generating an invoice

   □ The ability to manage buyers (create, read, update, and delete)

   □ The ability to see a list of bank accounts and use it when generating an invoice

   □ The ability to manage his/her own bank accounts (create, read, update, and delete)

   □ The ability to edit personal details and use them when generating an invoice

   Of course, we may want to have more functions, but this is enough for demonstrating how to design an application using the MVC pattern.

3. Next, we architect an application using the MVC pattern.

   After we have defined the features of our application, we need to understand what is more related to the model (business logic) and what is more related to the view (presentation). Let's split the functionality into several parts.

4. Then, we learn how to define models.

   Models present data and provide data-specific business logic. Models can be related to each other. In our case, they are as follows:

   □ InvoiceModel

   □ InvoiceItemModel

- ❑ BuyerModel
- ❑ SellerModel
- ❑ BankAccountModel

5. Then, will define collections of models.

   Our application allows users to operate on a number of models, so they need to be organized into a special iterable object named Collection. We need the following collections:

   - ❑ InvoiceCollection
   - ❑ InvoiceItemCollection
   - ❑ BuyerCollection
   - ❑ BankAccountCollection

6. Next, we define views.

   View present a model or a collection to the application user. A single model or collection can be rendered to be used by multiple views. The views that we need in our application are as follows:

   - ❑ EditInvoiceFormView
   - ❑ InvoicePageView
   - ❑ InvoiceListView
   - ❑ PrintInvoicePageView
   - ❑ EmailInvoiceFormView
   - ❑ YearlyIncomeGraphView
   - ❑ EditBuyerFormView
   - ❑ BuyerPageView
   - ❑ BuyerListView
   - ❑ EditBankAccountFormView
   - ❑ BankAccountPageView
   - ❑ BankAccountListView
   - ❑ EditSellerInfoFormView
   - ❑ ViewSellectInfoPageView
   - ❑ ConfirmationDialogView

7. Finally, we define a controller.

   A controller allows users to interact with an application. In MVC, each view can have a different controller that is used to do following:

   - ❑ Map a URL to a specific view
   - ❑ Fetch models from a server
   - ❑ Show and hide views
   - ❑ Handle user input

Defining business logic with models and collections

Now, it is time to design business logic for the Billing Application using the MVC and OOP approaches.

In this recipe, we are going to define an internal structure for our application with model and collection objects. Although a model represents a single object, a collection is a set of models that can be iterated, filtered, and sorted.

Relations between models and collections in the Billing Application conform to the following scheme:

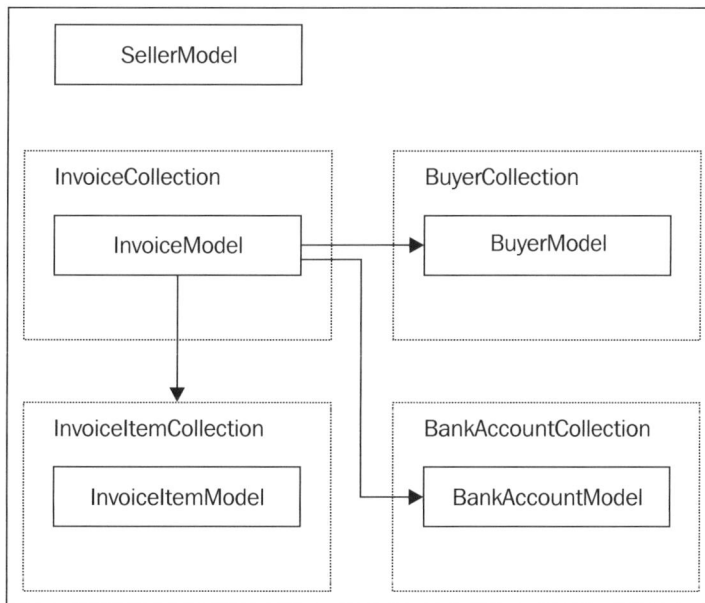

How to do it...

For each model, we are going to create two tables: one for properties and another for methods:

1. We define BuyerModel properties.

Name	Type	Required	Unique
id	Integer	Yes	Yes
name	Text	Yes	
address	Text	Yes	
phoneNumber	Text	No	

2. Then, we define SellerModel properties.

Name	Type	Required	Unique
id	Integer	Yes	Yes
name	Text	Yes	
address	Text	Yes	
phoneNumber	Text	No	
taxDetails	Text	Yes	

3. After this, we define BankAccountModel properties.

Name	Type	Required	Unique
id	Integer	Yes	Yes
beneficiary	Text	Yes	
beneficiaryAccount	Text	Yes	
bank	Text	Yes	
SWIFT	Text	Yes	
specialInstructions	Text	No	

4. We define InvoiceItemModel properties.

Name	Arguments	Return Type	Unique
calculateAmount	-	Decimal	

5. Next, we define InvoiceItemModel methods.

   We don't need to store the item amount in the model, because it always depends on the price and the quantity, so it can be calculated.

Name	Type	Required	Unique
id	Integer	Yes	Yes
deliveryDate	Date	Yes	
description	Text	Yes	
price	Decimal	Yes	
quantity	Decimal	Yes	

6. Now, we define InvoiceModel properties.

Name	Type	Required	Unique
id	Integer	Yes	Yes
referenceNumber	Text	Yes	
date	Date	Yes	
bankAccount	Reference	Yes	
items	Collection	Yes	
comments	Text	No	
status	Integer	Yes	

7. We define InvoiceModel methods.

   The invoice amount can easily be calculated as the sum of invoice item amounts.

Name	Arguments	Return Type	Unique
calculateAmount		Decimal	

8. Finally, we define collections.

   In our case, they are InvoiceCollection, InvoiceItemCollection, BuyerCollection, and BankAccountCollection. They are used to store models of an appropriate type and provide some methods to add/remove models to/from the collections.

How it works...

Models in Backbone.js are implemented by extending Backbone.Model, and collections are made by extending Backbone.Collection. To implement relations between models and collections, we can use special Backbone extensions, which are described in the later chapters of this book.

See also

▶ The *Operating with model attributes* recipe in *Chapter 2*, *Models*

▶ The *Creating a collection of models* recipe in *Chapter 3*, *Collections*

To learn more about object properties, methods, and OOP programming in JavaScript, you can refer to the following resource:

```
https://developer.mozilla.org/en-US/docs/JavaScript/Introduction_to_
Object-Oriented_JavaScript
```

Modeling an application's behavior with views and a router

Unlike traditional MVC frameworks, Backbone does not provide any distinct object that implements controller functionality. Instead, the controller is diffused between Backbone. Router and Backbone. View and the following is done:

> ▶ A router handles URL changes and delegates application flow to a view. Typically, the router fetches a model from the storage asynchronously. When the model is fetched, it triggers a view update.

> ▶ A view listens to DOM events and either updates a model or navigates an application through a router.

The following diagram shows a typical workflow in a Backbone application:

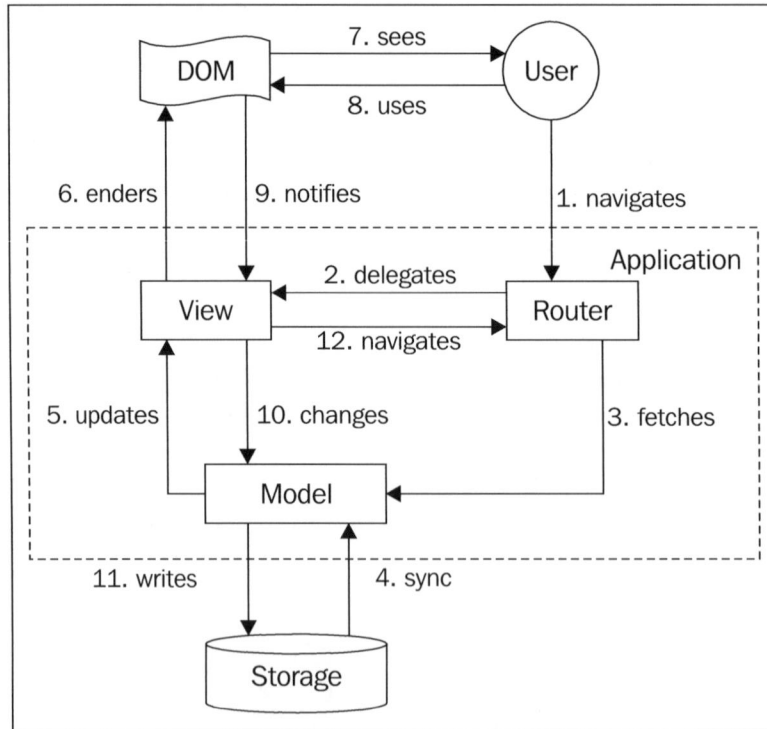

How to do it...

Let's follow the ensuing steps to understand how to define basic views and a router in our application:

1. First, we need to create wireframes for an application.

   Let's draw a couple of wireframes in this recipe:

   ❑ The Edit Invoice page allows users to select a buyer, to select the seller's bank account from the lists, to enter the invoice's date and a reference number, and to build a table of shipped products and services.

Edit Invoice

1. Select a buyer

John Smith ∨

2. Select bank account

Bank of Columbus ∨

3. Select currency

$ - USD ∨

4. Enter details

Date   Text

Ref #   Text

Comments

5. Enter product or services

Date	Description	Quan...	Price	Amount	
24 April, 2013	Wooden Toy House	3	22	66	⊖
24 April, 2013	Farm Animal Set	1	17	17	⊖

Add Item   **AMOUNT DUE** $ 83

Preview

▶ The Preview Invoice page shows how the final invoice will be seen by a buyer. This display should render all the information we have entered in the Edit Invoice form. Buyer and seller information can be looked up in the application storage. The user has the option to either go back to the Edit display or save this invoice.

Preview Invoice

North American Veeblefetzer   INVOICE

Beneficiary	Beneficiary Account	Bank	SWIFT
North American Veeblefetzer 185 West 74th Street New York, New York United States	2000 4638 1116 1420	Bank of Columbus 320 Fowler Street Lynbrook, New York United States	BNCLMB11

Bill To   **Comments**

John Smith
712 Red Bark Lane,
Henderson, Clark County, Nevada 89011
United States

Product or services

Date	Description	Quantity	Price	Amount
24 April, 2013	Wooden Toy House	3	22	66
24 April, 2013	Farm Animal Set	1	17	17

AMOUNT DUE $ 83

[Back]   [Save]

2. Then, we will define view objects.

According to the previous wireframes, we need to have two main views: EditInvoiceFormView and PreviewInvoicePageView. These views will operate with InvoiceModel; it refers to other objects, such as BankAccountModel and InvoiceItemCollection.

3. Now, we will split views into subviews.

   For each item in the Products or Services table, we may want to recalculate the Amount field depending on what the user enters in the Price and Quantity fields. The first way to do this is to re-render the entire view when the user changes the value in the table; however, it is not an efficient way, and it takes a significant amount of computer power to do this.

   We don't need to re-render the entire view if we want to update a small part of it. It is better to split the big view into different, independent pieces, such as subviews, that are able to render only a specific part of the big view. In our case, we can have the following views:

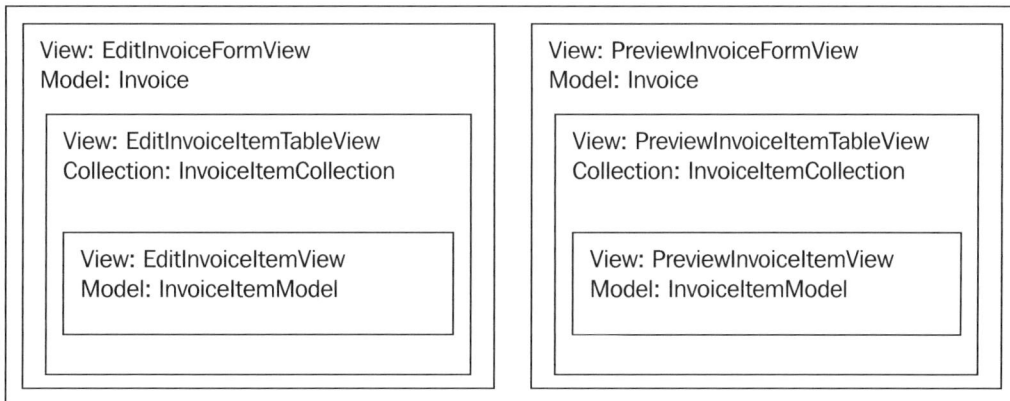

```
View: EditInvoiceFormView                    View: PreviewInvoiceFormView
Model: Invoice                               Model: Invoice

    View: EditInvoiceItemTableView               View: PreviewInvoiceItemTableView
    Collection: InvoiceItemCollection            Collection: InvoiceItemCollection


        View: EditInvoiceItemView                    View: PreviewInvoiceItemView
        Model: InvoiceItemModel                      Model: InvoiceItemModel
```

   As we can see, EditInvoiceItemTableView and PreviewInvoiceItemTableView render InvoiceItemCollection with the help of the additional views EditInvoiceItemView and PreviewInvoiceItemView that render InvoiceItemModel. Such separation allows us to re-render an item inside a collection when it is changed.

4. Finally, we will define URL paths that will be associated with a corresponding view. In our case, we can have several URLs to show different views, for example:

   ❑ /invoice/add

   ❑ /invoice/:id/edit

   ❑ /invoice/:id/preview

   Here, we assume that the Edit Invoice view can be used for either creating a new invoice or editing an existing one. In the router implementation, we can load this view and show it on specific URLs.

How it works...

The Backbone.View object can be extended to create our own view that will render model data. In a view, we can define handlers to user actions, such as data input and keyboard or mouse events.

In the application, we can have a single Backbone.Router object that allows users to navigate through an application by changing the URL in the address bar of the browser. The router object contains a list of available URLs and callbacks. In a callback function, we can trigger the rendering of a specific view associated with a URL.

If we want a user to be able to jump from one view to another, we may want him/her to either click on regular HTML links associated with a view or navigate to an application programmatically.

See also

▶ *Chapter 2*, Views

Creating an application structure from scratch

In this recipe, we are going to talk about how to create a Backbone project from scratch. There is important information of which we should be aware when dealing with the later chapters of this book.

How to do it...

We are going to speak about Backbone dependencies and the directory structure for our project. Let's follow the ensuing guidelines:

1. Download Backbone.js.

    Visit `http://backbone.js` and download the Backbone.js library. There are several versions available: production, development, and an edge version.

    You can use the production version for the best performance because it has been optimized and minimized. The development version may be good to use when working on the application, so you can use the code completion and debugging features of your IDE. And finally, you can use the edge version of Backbone, but do it at your own risk, because it may not be fully tested.

2. Download Backbone dependencies.

    Backbone.js depends on the Underscore.js library, which can be downloaded from `http://underscorejs.org`. Underscore is also shipped in three different versions.

    Also, Backbone.js depends on either the jQuery or Zepto libraries. These libraries have the same syntax and both provide useful functionality to the developer. They simplify work with the document tree, event handling, AJAX, and JavaScript animations.

    For many examples in this book, we are going to use the jQuery library, which can be downloaded from `http://jquery.com`. It is provided with both the development and production versions.

3. Create a project directory structure.

    If you follow a specific directory structure, it would be easier to find any file and work with it, because such an application structure brings more order into your project. Here is an example of a directory structure that can be used by a simple Backbone application:

    - lib/: This is a directory for third-party libraries, such as the following:

      backbone.js: This is the source code of Backbone.js

      underscore.js: This is the source code of Underscore.js

      jquery.js: This has sources of jQuery

    - js/: This is the directory of the project's JavaScript files.

      main.js: This is the main JavaScript file that has been used in the project

      index.html: This is the main file of our application.

    Create the main file of the application, which is index.html. It should include third-party libraries and your application files, as shown in the following code:

```
<!DOCTYPE html>
<html>
  <head>
    <meta charset="utf-8">
    <title>Backbone.js Cookbook - Application Template</title>

    <script src="lib/jquery.js"></script>
    <script src="lib/underscore.js"></script>
    <script src="lib/backbone.js"></script>

    <script src="js/main.js"></script>
  </head>
```

```
    <body></body>

</html>
```

4. Create the main JavaScript file named main.js that will contain the code of your application.

```
(function ($) {

    // Your code is here

}) (jQuery);
```

As we include our scripts into the head tag, they are executed before the body content is processed by a browser and before the whole HTML document is loaded.

In a Backbone application, as in many other JavaScript applications, we want to make sure our program starts to run right after the document is loaded, so main.js should look like the following code snippet:

```
(function ($) {

    // Object declarations goes here

    $(document).ready(function () {

        // Start application code goes here

    });
}) (jQuery);
```

> You can use this application template for creating your own Backbone app. We are also going to use this template for the examples in this book.

Writing your first Backbone application

In this recipe, we are going to write our first Backbone application. Let it be a simple part of the billing system.

For example, we can implement a model and a view for the invoice item. Let's create InvoiceItemModel that contains the Quantity and Price fields and calculates the item's amount. We also need to have PreviewInvoiceItemView that is used to render a model.

The output of our demo application could be very simple, as shown in the following screenshot:

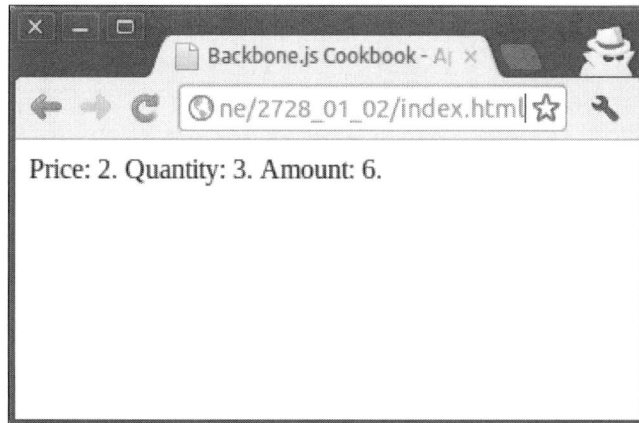

How to do it...

The new code in this recipe should go into the main.js file that we created in the previous recipe; we will do this as follows:

1. Define the model by extending it from the Backbone.Model object.

    ```
    var InvoiceItemModel = Backbone.Model.extend({

      // Set default values.
      defaults: {
        price: 0,
        quantity: 0
      },

      // Calculate amount.
      calculateAmount: function() {
        return this.get('price') * this.get('quantity');
      }
    });
    ```

    In the InvoiceItemModel object, we have initialized the default values and performed the business logic, a function that calculates the total amount.

2. Create a model instance.

    ```
    var invoiceItemModel = new InvoiceItemModel({
      price: 2,
      quantity: 3
    });
    ```

3. Define the view that will render the model.

```
var PreviewInvoiceItemView = Backbone.View.extend({

    // Define template using templating engine from
    // Underscore.js.
    template: _.template('\
      Price: <%= price %>.\
      Quantity: <%= quantity %>.\
      Amount: <%= amount %>.\
    '),

    // Render view.
    render: function () {

        // Generate HTML by rendering the template.
        var html = this.template({

            // Pass model properties to the template.
            price: this.model.get('price'),
            quantity: this.model.get('quantity'),

            // Calculate amount and pass it to the template.
            amount: this.model.calculateAmount()
        });

        // Set html for the view element using jQuery.
        $(this.el).html(html);
    }
});
```

As we can see, our view uses the this.model and this.el properties that are passed to the view when it is created.

```
var previewInvoiceItemView = new PreviewInvoiceItemView({
    model: invoiceItemModel,
    el: 'body'
});
```

Inside a view, we used the jQuery library to set the content for the element associated with the view $(this.el).html(html). In our case, this.el contains 'body' that is also a jQuery selector.

Such selectors are similar to CSS selectors and allow jQuery to find an arbitrary HTML element using the $() function.

4. To render a view, we simply need to execute the render() method.

    ```
    previewInvoiceItemVicw.rcnder();
    ```

    When rendering a view, we also used a templating engine provided by Underscore.
    js. This templating engine substitutes templates with data and outputs static HTML.
    More information about templates is available in the Using templates in a view recipe
    of *Chapter 6*, Templates, Forms, and UX Sugar.

5. Start the application.

    There are several ways to start an application. If your application has only a single
    view, you can create a new instance of it and render it manually.

    An application should be started right after the HTML page is loaded. Let's write
    some code that will start a simple Backbone application:

    ```
    // When document is ready create the Model and show
    // the View.
    $(document).ready(function () {

      // Create InvoiceItemModel instance and set
      // model attributes.
      var invoiceItemModel = new InvoiceItemModel({
        price: 2,
        quantity: 3
      });

      // Create PreviewInvoiceItemView instance.
      var previewInvoiceItemView = new PreviewInvoiceItemView({

        // Pass our model.
        model: invoiceItemModel,

        // Set element where to render HTML.
        el: 'body'
      });

      // Render view manually.
      previewInvoiceItemView.render();
    });
    ```

See also

*   ▶ *Chapter 2*, Models
*   ▶ *Chapter 3*, Collections
*   ▶ *Chapter 4*, Views
*   ▶ *Chapter 5*, Events and Bindings

Implementing URL routing in your application

The Backbone.Router object is used for navigation inside your application. You should use it if you want to access different view pages by hitting the appropriate URLs. Users can also navigate through an application using the browser's history bar.

By default, the router works well with hash paths, such as index.html#path/to/page. Any string that is placed after a hash character is supposed to be a route and is processed by Backbone.Router.

How to do it...

Here, we are going to explain how to create our own router in our application:

1. Define a router by extending Backbone.Router into the Workspace object and setting pairs of routes and callback functions for them inside the routes property that is passed to the extend() method. This gives the router information of which callback should be executed in case the appropriate route is accessed.

```
var Workspace = Backbone.Router.extend({
  routes: {
    // Default path.
    '': 'invoiceList',

    // Usage of static path.
    'invoice': 'invoiceList',
  },
});
```

2. Add a callback method to the router object.

```
invoiceList: function() {
  var invoiceListView = new InvoiceListView({
    el: 'body'
  });
  invoiceListView.render();
}
```

If the user visits index.html or index.html#invoice, the invoiceList() callback is executed, which renders InvoiceListView. Here, InvoiceListView is a simple stub.

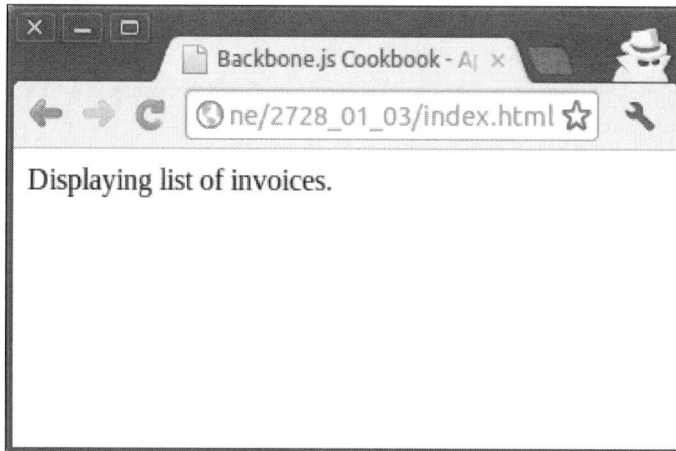

Displaying list of invoices.

3. Tell Backbone to use this router and start the application.

```
$(document).ready(function () {
  new Workspace();
  Backbone.history.start();
});
```

Here, we create a new Workspace object and execute the start() method of the Backbone.history object that is used for global application routing. As always, we should start our application right after the HTML page has loaded completely.

How it works...

Backbone.Router is used just for defining routes and callbacks. All the important jobs are done by Backbone.history that serves as a global router (per frame) to handle hashchange or pushState events, match the appropriate route, and trigger callbacks. You shouldn't ever have to create an instance of the global router—you should use the reference to Backbone. history that will be created for you automatically if you make use of routers with routes.

There's more...

Backbone router allows the defining of routes with parameters, which we are going to explain in this section.

Parsing parameters in a URL

If we want the router to parse parameters in a URL, we need to use the colon character (:) before the parameter's name. Here is an example that demonstrates how Backbone.Router parses URLs with a parameter.

```
var Workspace = Backbone.Router.extend({
  routes: {
    // Usage of fragment parameter.
    'invoice/:id': 'invoicePage',
  },

  // Shows invoice page.
  invoicePage: function(id) {
    var invoicePageView = new InvoicePageView({
      el: 'body',

      // Pass parameter to the view.
      id: id
    });
    invoicePageView.render();
  },
});
```

Paths such as index.html#invoice/1 and index.html#invoice/2 will be parsed by a router. In both cases, the invoicePage() callback is executed; it passes the ID parameter to InvoiceLPageView and renders it.

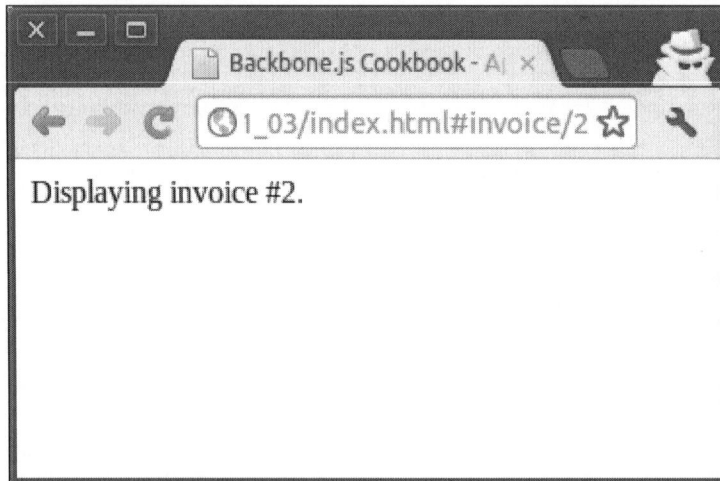

Validate parameters in your router

There is no default way to set a restriction for the data type or format of the parameters inside the routes definition. All parameters that are passed to the router callbacks are strings, and it is up to the developer to validate them.

See also

▶ The Handling router events recipe in *Chapter 5*, Events and Bindings

▶ The Switching views using Backbone.Router recipe in *Chapter 4*, Views

Extending an application with plugins

Backbone's core is small, well-tested, and nicely maintained. However, developers may need additional functionalities to be used by a complex web application. The power of the Backbone framework depends on modularity and flexibility. Existing components can easily be either extended or replaced; thus, many developers create their own plugins.

There are over 100 plugins that can be downloaded and used in your application from `https://github.com/documentcloud/backbone/wiki/Extensions,-Plugins, -Resources`. In this book, we are going to use some of them, so we need to know how to extend our application with plugins.

How to do it...

If the plugin is a single JavaScript file, simply copy it into the lib folder of the project and include it in index.html.

```
<script src="lib/backbone.plugin.js"></script>
```

Alternatively, if the plugin has been shipped with additional files, such as CSS and images, place all the plugin files in the plugin-name directory under the lib folder, and then include the JS and CSS files in index.html.

Use Git submodules

If your project is hosted in the Git repository, you can use the Git submodule command to insert a plugin repository inside your project repository. This is very useful if you want to have an easy way to update your project plugins by writing a single git command.

► The Creating a Backbone.js extension with Grunt recipe in *Chapter 8,
Special Techniques*

Contributing to the Backbone project

Backbone.js is an open source project that has been developed by a strong community.
In this recipe, we are going to speak about things that will help you became a part of this
community and improve Backbone.js.

How to do it...

Let's follow the ensuing steps to make Backbone.js better:

1. Work on the issue queue.

   If you found a bug in Backbone.js or want a new feature to be implemented, you can
   submit your issue to the issue queue at `https://github.com/documentcloud/`
   `backbone/issues`. Before doing this, make sure there is no similar issue;
   otherwise, you can update the existing issue queue.

2. Contribute code.

   You can submit your own code to the Backbone project. Such a contribution can be
   very helpful to the community and the project itself.

   By using Backbone, you save your own time. By contributing to the project, you save
   the time of other developers who use it and your own time in the future instead of
   having to work on the same issue again.

   Detailed guidelines for the code contributing process can be found on the wiki page
   at `https://github.com/documentcloud/backbone/wiki/Contributing-`
   `to-Backbone`.

3. Work on the documentation of Backbone.js.

   The official documentation, which is located at `http://backbonejs.org`, is
   based on a recent version of Backbone.js in the GitHub repository. You can improve
   the documentation by either updating the index.html file or the docs directory. If you
   want to add a new example, use the examples folder.

2
Models

In this chapter, we will cover:

- ▶ Creating a model
- ▶ Operating with model attributes
- ▶ Operating with model identifier
- ▶ Validating model attributes
- ▶ Overriding getters and setters
- ▶ Creating undo points to store/restore a model's state
- ▶ Implementing workflow for a model
- ▶ Using advanced validation in a model
- ▶ Validating an HTML form
- ▶ Working with nested attributes in a model
- ▶ Implementing a one-to-one relationship

Introduction

In this chapter we are going to learn what a Backbone model is and how can we use it. We are also going to consider various Backbone extensions, which provide lots of improvement and bring amazing features to our models.

The first three recipes of the current chapter contain information for beginners who are not familiar with Backbone yet; and other recipes bring additional value and cover more advanced topics.

Creating a model

A model is a building brick of any MVC application, which contains data, provides validation, performs access control, and implements specific business logic required by an application. In `Backbone.js`, a model is defined by extending its instance from the `Backbone.Model` object. In this recipe, we are going to learn how to work with models in `Backbone.js`.

How to do it...

Perform the following steps to define a new model object and create its instance:

1. Define a model by extending `Backbone.Model`.

   ```
   var InvoiceItemModel = Backbone.Model.extend({

   });
   ```

   There is no need to define a data structure inside the model object, because Backbone allows it to be defined dynamically when the model is initialized.

2. Create a `Backbone.Model` instance and initialize it with attribute values.

   ```
   var invoiceItemModel = new InvoiceItemModel({
      date: '2013-04-24',
      description: 'Wooden Toy House',
      price: 22,
      quantity: 3
   });
   ```

There's more...

In this section, we are going to learn how to clone a model and how to initialize a model with default values.

Cloning a model

When you assign a model to another variable, it makes one model reflect changes in another model. If you need an independent copy of a model, use the `clone()` method.

```
newModel = invoiceItemModel.clone();
```

Setting default attribute values

Sometimes, you may want your model to have attributes that are initialized with default values when a new model instance is created, so you don't need to set them manually. Here is how default attributes are defined:

```
var InvoiceItemModel = Backbone.Model.extend({

  // Define default attributes.
  defaults: {
    date: '',
    description: '',
    price: 0,
    quantity: 1
  },
});
```

The following example shows that the `quantity` and `date` attributes are initialized by default:

```
var invoiceItemModel2 = new InvoiceItemModel({
  description: 'Farm Animal Set',
  price: 17
});

invoiceItemModel2.get('date') != undefined; // true
invoiceItemModel2.get('quantity'); // 1
```

Setting default attribute values with a multiline expression

If you want to set default values with a multiline expression you can wrap it into a function and call it when setting default attributes in `defaults`.

```
// Create new model object
var InvoiceItemModel = Backbone.Model.extend({

  // Set default attributes.
  defaults: {
    description: '',
    price: 0,
    quantity: 1,

  // Use function for multiline expression.
    date: function() {
      var date = new Date();

    // Return attribute value.
      return date.toISOString();
    }
  }
});
```

There is also a way to do the same in the `initialize()` method, which is called right after the model object is created and initialized with values.

```
// Crate new model
var InvoiceItemModel = Backbone.Model.extend({

    // Set default values.
    defaults: {
        description: '',
        price: 0,
        quantity: 1,
    },

    // Set default values in initialize method.
    // Following method is run after the object is created.
    initialize: function() {

        // Check that attribute is not initialized yet.
        if (!this.has('date')) {
            var date = new Date();

        // Set attribute value.
            this.set('date', date.toISOString());
        }
    }
}
```

In the `initialize()` method we set the `date` attribute to today's date using JavaScript's `Date` object. Before doing this, we need to check that the `date` attribute is not initialized yet, so we do not override it.

If the default attributes are defined, then they can override the attributes defined in the `initialize()` method, and so we need to remove such attributes from the `default` values, otherwise they are initialized as defaults instead.

See also

▶ In the current recipe examples, we used the `has()` and `set()` methods, which are described in the following recipe: *Operating with model attributes*

Operating with model attributes

Attributes are where a model stores all its data. Unlike model properties, which are used for storing internal object information, attributes cannot be accessed via the `.` operator. There are special methods to work with them, which we are going to learn in this recipe.

How to do it...

The main methods to work with model attributes are `get()`, `set()`, `unset()`, and `clear()`.

1. Use the `get()` method to get an attribute value.

   ```
   var quantity = invoiceItemModel.get('quantity');
   ```

   If the attribute is not found, `undefined` is returned.

2. Use the `set()` method to update/create a single attribute value.

   ```
   invoiceItemModel.set('quantity', 5);
   ```

   ❑ To update multiple attributes use key-value format.

   ```
   invoiceItemModel.set({
     quantity: 5,
     price: 10
   });
   ```

   When setting an attribute if it does not exist, one is created. The `set()` method returns a reference with the value `true` to the model, if validation does not fail; otherwise returns the value `false`. We will learn more about validation in the recipe, *Validating model attributes*.

3. Use the `unset()` method to delete an attribute from a model.

   ```
   invoiceItemModel.unset('quantity');
   ```

4. Use the `clear()` method to delete all attributes from a model.

   ```
   invoiceItemModel.clear();
   ```

How it works...

Attributes are stored in the `attributes` property. It is better not to access attributes directly and to use methods we have learned previously; otherwise, it can break the event triggering mechanism or integration with other Backbone extensions.

When a new module is initialized, values from the `defaults` property are assigned to the `attributes` one.

There's more...

In this section we are going to learn some useful methods with the model attributes.

Checking if a model has an attribute

To check if a model has an attribute, use the `has()` method. It returns `true` if the attribute exists, otherwise `false`.

```
if (!invoiceItemModel.has('quantity')) {
  console.log('Quantity attribute does not exists!')
}
```

Getting HTML escaped attribute value

If you are going to display user-entered text, which you assume is in plain text format, you should worry about security issues. The best way to prevent vulnerability which may lead to possible XSS attacks is to use the `escape()` method before outputting any user entered text. This disallows the browser to parse any HTML code by escaping HTML characters. Let's figure out how it works:

```
var hacker = new Backbone.Model({
  name: "<script>alert('xss')</script>"
});
var escaped_name = hacker.escape('name');
// &lt;script&gt;alert(&#x27;xss&#x27;)&lt;&#x2F;script&gt;
```

Operating with the model identifier

Each model has a unique identifier property ID, which allows distinguishing one model from another. When developing a Backbone application it is often required to operate with an identifier.

How to do it...

The following steps explains how to set and get the `id` property:

1. Setting and getting the `id` property is really easy.

    ```
    invoiceItemModel.id =
      Math.random().toString(36).substr(2);
    ```

    Getting the id property looks as follows:

    ```
    var id = invoiceItemModel.id;
    ```

How it works...

The `id` property provides direct access to an attribute where the identifier is stored. By default it is `id`; however, you can override it by setting `idAttribute` when extending a model.

```
var Meal = Backbone.Model.extend({
  idAttribute: "_id"
});
```

When a new model is created, the identifier is empty unless it is manually assigned.

There's more...

If `id` is not initialized yet in your model, then you can use a client identifier, which can be accessed using the `cid` property. The value of `cid` is unique and assigned automatically when a new model instance is created. Client IDs can take forms, such as `c0`, `c1`, `c2`, and so on.

Validating model attributes

To prevent unexpected behavior, we often need to validate model attributes.

How to do it...

Perform the following steps to set up an attribute validation:

1. Validation can be done by defining the `validate()` method.

```
var InvoiceItemModel = Backbone.Model.extend({

  // Define validation criteria.
  validate: function(attrs) {
    if (attrs.quantity <= 0) {
      return "quantity can't be negative or equal to
        zero";
    }
  }
});
```

The `attrs` parameter contains the attribute values that were changed. The `validate()` method will return an error message if they do not validate.

2. Attribute validation is triggered on the `save()` method. It can also trigger on the `set()` method if you pass {validate: true} as the last parameter.

```
var invoiceItemModel = new InvoiceItemModel({
  description: 'Wooden Toy House',
  price: 10
});

  // Set value that is not valid.
  invoiceItemModel.set('quantity', -1, {validate: true});
```

> When validating a model you can still access old attribute values with the help of `this.get()` or `this.attributes`.

How it works...

`validate` is called before `save()`, and accepts the updated model attributes, which are passed from `save()`. If `validate()` returns an error string, `save()` will not continue, and the model attributes will not be modified. Failed validation triggers the `invalid` event. If you want validation to be triggered in the `set()` method, pass {validate: true} as the last parameter.

There's more...

In this section, we are going to investigate more details about validation.

Handling validation errors

If a model does not validate, we often need to continue running an application and provide a custom code for handling events. Let's check out how it is done.

```
invoiceItemModel.on("invalid", function(model, error) {
  console.log(error);
});
```

Such an error handler should be bound before the validation event is triggered.

There is also another way of handling events, which allows us to pass an error handling function as an option to the `set()`, `fetch()`, `save()`, or `destroy()` methods.

```
var invoiceItemModel2 = new InvoiceItemModel({
  description: 'Animal Farm',
  price: 17
});
  invoiceItemModel2.set({quantity: 0}, {
```

```
    invalid: function(model, error) {
      console.log(error);
    },
    validate: true
  });
```

Triggering validation manually

Though validation is performed every time a model is updated or saved to the storage, sometimes you may want to check manually if the model validates. Let's figure out how to do it.

```
var invoiceItemModel3 = new InvoiceItemModel({
  description: 'Wooden Toy House',
  price: 10,
  quantity: -5
});
  invoiceItemModel3.isValid(); // false
```

isValid() returns true or false, but does not trigger the invalid event.

See also

  ▸ *Handling events of Backbone objects* in *Chapter 5, Events and Bindings*

Overriding getters and setters

Sometimes it is required to override getters or setters in your application. There can be different reasons to do so:

  ▸ An attribute is stored in a different format rather than a format for input or output

  ▸ You have a virtual attribute that is not stored in the model, but depends on other attributes

  ▸ Prevent illegal values to be assigned to an attribute

By default, Backbone does not allow users to override getters or setters, but there is an extension named Backbone.Mutators, which allows you to do so.

Getting ready

There is a link to download Backbone.Mutators from the **GitHub** page https://github.com/asciidisco/Backbone.Mutators.

To include this extension into your project, save the `backbone.mutators.js` file into the `lib` folder and include a reference to it in `index.html`.

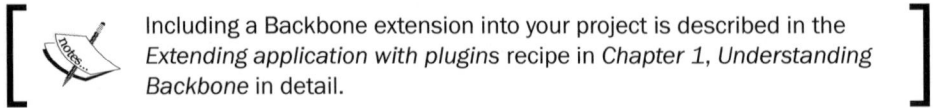

> Including a Backbone extension into your project is described in the *Extending application with plugins* recipe in *Chapter 1, Understanding Backbone* in detail.

How to do it...

We can specify a getter or setter for a virtual attribute that does not exist. This can be helpful in some cases, for example, if a virtual attribute depends on other attributes.

1. Introduce a new virtual attribute by overriding getter for it.

```
var BuyerModel = Backbone.Model.extend({

  // Use mutators
  mutators: {

  // Introduce virtual attribute.
    fullName: {
      get: function () {
        return this.firstName + ' ' + this.lastName;
      }
    }
  }
});
```

In the model object, we defined a new `mutators` attribute, which provides our model with a getter for the new virtual attribute named `fullName`. This attribute is not assumed to be stored in the model, because it contains values of existing attributes `firstName` and `lastName`. Now, let's see how we can use an overridden getter.

```
var buyerModel = new BuyerModel();
buyerModel.set({
  firstName: 'John',
  lastName: 'Smith'
});

buyerModel.get('fullName'); // John Smith
buyerModel.get('firstName'); // John
buyerModel.get('lastName'); // Smith
```

2. Override setter, so the virtual attribute is not actually saved in the model, but other attributes are updated instead.

```
var BuyerModel = Backbone.Model.extend({

    // Use mutators
    mutators: {

        // Introduce virtual attribute.
        fullName: {
            set: function (key, value, options, set) {
                var names = value.split(' ');
                this.set('firstName', names[0], options);
                this.set('lastName', names[1], options);
            }
        }
    }
});
```

In the setter for the `fullName` attribute, we split a value into an array and then assign the `firstName` and `lastName` attributes with its parts. Here is an example which demonstrates how it can be used:

```
var buyerModel2 = new BuyerModel()
buyerModel2.set('fullName', 'Joe Bloggs');

buyerModel2.get('fullName'); // Joe Bloggs
buyerModel2.get('firstName'); // Joe
buyerModel2.get('lastName'); // Bloggs
```

Initialize attributes using the set() method

If you use setter mutator for an attribute, the only way to trigger it is to call the `set()` method. Setter mutator won't work if you assign attributes when creating a new model, because in this case the `change` event is not triggered. Otherwise, you need to trigger the `change` event for a specific property.

How it works...

The `Backbone.Mutators` extension overrides the `get()` and `set()` methods of `Bakcbone.Model`. New methods try to call overridden getters and setters. If not, run the original `get()` or `set()` methods.

It also overrides the `toJSON()` method and replaces attributes which have overridden getter.

There's more...

In this section, we are going to learn the advanced usage of the `Backbone.Mutators` extension.

Overriding getter and setter of an existing attribute

Overriding setter of an existing attribute may be done if you need the attribute to be stored in a different format rather than the one in which it is outputted or inputted. You can override getter and setter for this attribute and solve this problem. Let's see how to use `Backbone.Mutators` for existing attributes:

```
var BuyerModel = Backbone.Model.extend({

  // Use mutators.
  mutators: {

    // Override existing attribute.
    vip: {
      get: function() {
        return this.vip === true ? 'VIP' : 'Regular';
      },
      set: function (key, value, options, set) {
        set(key, value === 'VIP', options);
      }
    }
  }
});
```

In this model, there is the `vip` attribute, which is `boolean`. We want this attribute to be represented as a string to the user, so we are going to override getter and setter for it.

The usage syntax stays the same as for a regular attribute.

```
var buyerModel3 = new BuyerModel();
buyerModel2.set({
  fullName: 'Mister X',
  vip: 'VIP'
});

buyerModel2.get('vip'); // VIP
buyerModel2.attributes.vip; // true
```

Mutators aim to override setters or getters, but they do not modify attribute values itself. You can always get the original attributes by accessing the `attributes` property of a model.

Handling mutators events

You can bind callback to the `mutators:set:*` event. Here is how it is done:

```
buyerModel3.on('mutators:set:fullName',
  function (a, b, c, d) {
    console.log('mutators:set:fullName is triggered');
});

buyerModel3.set({
  fullName: 'Mister Y'
});
```

See also

▸ *Handling events of Backbone objects* in *Chapter 5, Events and Bindings*

Creating undo points to store/restore a model's state

Sometimes, you may need to manage the states of a model in your application. This can be useful in one of the following cases:

▸ Your application requires an undo/redo feature

▸ You want to implement transactions

▸ Your application emulates some process

▸ You want to change a model temporarily and then restore it

Typically for all of the previous cases developers often use the `Memento` pattern. There is an implementation of this pattern in Backbone, which is available in the `Backbone.Memento` extension. This extension allows developers to store or restore a model's state and provides a stack for operating with multiple states.

Getting ready

You can download the `Backbone.Memento` extension from the **GitHub** page `https://github.com/derickbailey/backbone.memento`. To include this extension into your project, save the `backbone.memento.js` file into the `lib` folder and include a reference to it in `index.html`.

> Including a Backbone extension into your project is described in the *Extending application with plugins* recipe in *Chapter 1, Understanding Backbone* in detail.

How to do it...

Perform the following steps to operate model states:

1. Extend a model with the `Backbone.Memento` extension in the `initialize()` method.

   ```
   var InvoiceItemModel = Backbone.Model.extend({

     // Extend model instance with memento instance.
     initialize: function() {
       _.extend(this, new Backbone.Memento(this));
     }
   });
   ```

2. Create the model instance and initialize it with values.

   ```
   var invoiceItemModel = new InvoiceItemModel();
   invoiceItemModel.set('price', 10);
   ```

3. Use the `store()` method to save a state.

   ```
   invoiceItemModel.store();
   ```

4. Update the model with temporary values.

   ```
   invoiceItemModel.set('price', 20);
   ```

5. Use the `restore()` method to retrieve a previously saved state.

   ```
   invoiceItemModel.restore();
   ```

6. Retrieve model values of the saved state.

   ```
   invoiceItemModel.get('price'); // 10
   ```

How it works...

Memento uses the **LIFO** (**last in, first out**) data structure, also known as stack, for storing model states. So it is possible to save model states multiple times, and then restore them in a backward direction. The following diagram shows how it works:

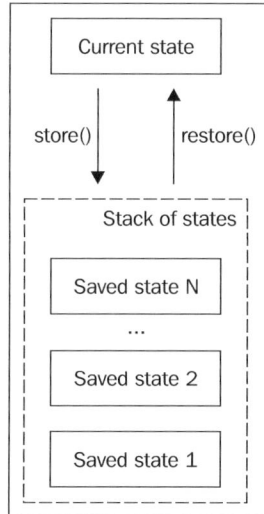

```
                    ┌──────────────────────────┐
                    │   ┌──────────────────┐    │
                    │   │  Current state   │    │
                    │   └──────────────────┘    │
                    │      │          ▲         │
                    │ store()       restore()   │
                    │      │          │         │
                    │      ▼          │         │
                    │  ┌ ─ ─ ─ ─ ─ ─ ─ ─ ─ ─ ┐  │
                    │    Stack of states       │
                    │  │ ┌──────────────────┐│  │
                    │    │  Saved state N   │  │
                    │  │ └──────────────────┘│  │
                    │           ...           │
                    │  │ ┌──────────────────┐│  │
                    │    │  Saved state 2   │  │
                    │  │ └──────────────────┘│  │
                    │    ┌──────────────────┐  │
                    │  │ │  Saved state 1   ││  │
                    │    └──────────────────┘  │
                    │  └ ─ ─ ─ ─ ─ ─ ─ ─ ─ ─ ┘  │
                    └──────────────────────────┘
```

Each time you call the `store()` method, the state is saved on top of the stack. Each time you call the `restore()` method, the state that was saved last is restored and deleted from the top of the stack.

There's more...

In this section, we are going to understand the advanced features of Memento.

Working with the Memento stack

Here is an example which demonstrates how to work with such stack of states:

```javascript
// States stack demo.
var invoiceItemModel2 = new InvoiceItemModel();
invoiceItemModel2.set('price', 10);

// Save state and update value.
invoiceItemModel2.store();
invoiceItemModel2.set('price', 20);

// Save state and update value.
invoiceItemModel2.store();
```

```
invoiceItemModel2.set('price', 30);

// Restore last state and get value.
invoiceItemModel2.restore();
invoiceItemModel2.get('price'); // 20

// Restore last state and get value.
invoiceItemModel2.restore();
invoiceItemModel2.get('price'); // 10
```

As we can see in the preceding code, dealing with stacks is quite easy.

Restoring from the first state in the stack

Sometimes, it is required to reset a model to the state in which it was first saved in the stack, no matter how many states were saved after. This can be done using the `restart()` method.

```
invoiceItemModel3.restart();
```

Ignoring attributes from being restored

There is an interesting feature in `Backbone.Memento`, which allows you to ignore some model attributes from being saved or restored. It is very useful if a model contains some technical properties, which is not intended to be used as part of the state. When extending a model in the `initialize()` method, pass the properties to be ignored in the `ignore` option.

```
var AnotherInvoiceItemModel = Backbone.Model.extend({

  // Extend model instance with memento instance.
  // Ignore restoring of description attribute.
  initialize: function() {
    _.extend(this, new Backbone.Memento(
      this, {ignore: ["description"]}
    ));
  }
});
```

Working with collections

The Memento extension also allows to extend a collection with Memento functionality. It provides the same methods when working with collections `store()`, `restore()`, and `restart()`.

See also

▸ There is also another extension named `Backbone.actAs.Mementoable`, which implements the Memento pattern in a more accurate way, because it uses separate objects for storing states. It is more flexible, but does not provide stack out of the box and cannot ignore specific attributes from being saved/restored.

▸ `Backbone.actAs.Mementoable` can be downloaded from the **GitHub** page `https://github.com/iVariable/Backbone.actAs.Mementoable`.

▸ You can learn more about working with collections in *Chapter 3, Collections*.

Implementing workflow for a model

If you are implementing a business logic, which assumes that a model can be in different states and there are special rules applied to a state change, you should use the `workflow.js` extension, which is very helpful for building such kind of functionality.

Getting ready

You can download the `workflow.js` extension from the GitHub page `https://github.com/kendagriff/workflow.js`. To include this extension into your project, save the `workflow.js` file into the `lib` folder and include a reference to it in `index.html`.

> Including a Backbone extension into your project is described in the *Extending application with plugins* recipe in *Chapter 1, Understanding Backbone* in detail.

How to do it...

Let's create a workflow for `InvoiceModel`, because it has a `status` attribute, which represents the model state and is well suited for a workflow example.

1. Draw a graph of the states and possible transitions.

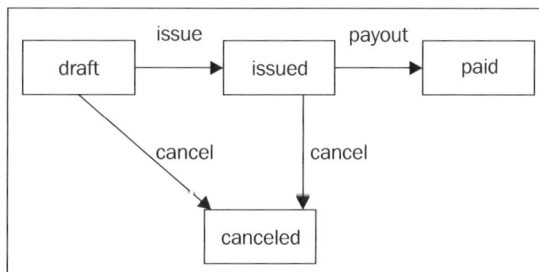

Available states are draft, issued, paid, and canceled. There are also a few transitions available that allow one state to be changed into another. If there is no appropriate transition, then such a change is not possible.

2. Define `workflow` in code.

```
var InvoiceModel = Backbone.Model.extend({

  // Define workflow states.
  workflow: {

    // Define initial state.
    initial: 'draft',

    // Define state transitions.
    events: [
      { name: 'issue', from: 'draft', to: 'issued' },
      { name: 'payout', from: 'issued', to: 'paid' },
      { name: 'cancel', from: 'draft', to: 'canceled' },
      { name: 'cancel', from: 'issued', to: 'canceled' },
    ]
  },

  initialize: function() {
    // Extend model instance with workflow instance.
    // Set attribute name which contains status.
    _.extend(this,
      new Backbone.Workflow(this, {attrName: 'status'})
    );
  }
});
```

As we can see, there is a new `workflow` property which describes our workflow. Transitions are defined in an array, which is assigned to the `events` property.

Each element of the transitions array should contain the name of the transition, from state, and to state. Initial state of the model should be defined in the `initial` property.

In the previous example, in the `initialize()` method, we extend our model object with an instance of the `Backbone.Workflow` object and pass the state attribute name (`attrName`) as an option, which contains `'status'` instead of the default value `'workflow_state'`.

3. Trigger workflow transition by calling the `triggerEvent()` method.

```
var invoiceModel = new InvoiceModel();
invoiceModel.get('status'); // draft
```

```
invoiceModel.triggerEvent('issue');
invoiceModel.get('status'); // issued

invoiceModel.triggerEvent('payout');
invoiceModel.get('status') // paid
```

As we can see in the preceding code, `triggerEvent()` accepts a single parameter, which is the transition name. In case if an inappropriate transition is triggered, then an exception is thrown.

How it works...

The `Workflow.js` extension is written on **CoffeeScript** and is quite easy to understand. It just provides the `triggerEvent()` method, which switches the `workflow` property and triggers an event.

There's more...

In this section, we are going to learn how to handle transition events.

Binding callbacks to transition events

Sometimes, you may want to execute a code when a specific transition is triggered. In this case, you need to bind a callback function to a transition event. This callback is executed if an event is being triggered.

`Workflow.js` provides two types of events `transition:from:*` and `transition:to:*`. The first one is triggered when a workflow loses a specific state, and the second one is triggered when a workflow reaches a specific state. Let's define event bindings for our model.

```
var InvoiceModel = Backbone.Model.extend({

  // Define workflow states.
  // [workflow definition goes here]

  initialize: function() {
    // Extend model instance with workflow instance.
    // Set attribute name which contains status.
    _.extend(this,
      new Backbone.Workflow(this, {attrName: 'status'})
    );

    // Bind reaction on event when status changes from
    // draft to any.
    this.bind('transition:from:draft', function() {
```

```
      this.set('createdDate', new Date().toISOString());
   });

   // Bind reaction on event when status changes
   // from any to paid.
   this.bind('transition:to:paid, function() {
      this.set('payoutDate', new Date().toISOString());
   });
 }
});
```

In the preceding example, we bind a couple of callbacks, which update date attributes when appropriate events are triggered.

The next code snippet is an example which demonstrates what happens when workflow events are triggered.

```
var invoiceModel = new InvoiceModel();
invoiceModel.get('status'); // draft

invoiceModel.triggerEvent('issue');
invoiceModel.get('status'); // issued
invoiceModel.get('createdDate');
// 2012-05-01T12:00:10.234Z

invoiceModel.triggerEvent('payout');
invoiceModel.get('status') // paid
invoiceModel.get('payoutDate');
// 2012-05-01T12:00:10.238Z
```

Always use the triggerEvent() method when changing state

Event callback is executed if an event is triggered by the `triggerEvent()` method only. That is why an event callback is not executed when an object is initialized or if you use the `set()` method to update the workflow state.

See also

▶ *Handling events of Backbone objects* in *Chapter 5, Events and Bindings*

Using advanced validation in a model

By default, Backbone provides a simple way for validating model attributes using the `validate()` method, which allows to create your own validating function, but this can take more developer's time compared to the usage of existing solutions.

Getting ready

Why don't you save time with another Backbone extension named `Backbone.Validation`, which provides lots of features and allows to reuse existing validators. It is available to download from the **GitHub** page `https://github.com/thedersen/backbone.validation`.

To include this extension into your project, save the `backbone-validation.js` file in the `lib` folder and include a reference to it in `index.html`.

> Including a Backbone extension into your project is described in the *Extending application with plugins* recipe in *Chapter 1, Understanding Backbone* in detail.

How to do it...

Perform the following steps to set the validation criteria for a model:

1. Extend `Backbone.object()` with `Backbone.Validation.mixin`.

   ```
   _.extend(Backbone.Model.prototype, Backbone.Validation.mixin);
   ```

   > There is more information about mixins in the *Using mixins with Backbone objects* recipe in *Chapter 8, Special Techniques*.

2. Define the validation criteria in the `validation` property.

   ```
   var BuyerModel = Backbone.Model.extend({

     // Defining a validation criteria.
     validation: {
       name: {
         required: true
       },
       email: {
         pattern: 'email'
       }
     }
   });
   ```

How it works...

The `Backbone.Validation` extension overrides the `validate()` method of `Backbone.Model`, so we can still call the `validate()` and `isValid()` methods as usual, and validation is performed automatically when a model is updated. Let's check this out.

```
var buyerModel = new BuyerModel();

// Set attribute values which do not validate.
buyerModel.set({
  email: 'http://example.com'
}, {validate: true});

// Check if model is valid.
buyerModel.isValid(); // false
buyerModel.get('email'); // undefined
```

There's more...

In this section, we are going to learn more about built-in validators.

Using built-in validators

In the previous example, we reused existing validators, such as `required` and `pattern`. They are named built-in validators. In this recipe, we are going to learn how to use all of them.

▶ **required**: It validates if the attribute is required or not. It can be equal to true or false.

```
var BuyerModel = Backbone.Model.extend({
  validation: {
    name: {
      required: true
    },
  }
});
```

▶ **acceptance**: It validates if something has to be accepted, for example, terms of use. It checks whether the attribute value is true or false. It works with `boolean` attributes.

```
var UserRegistrationModel = Backbone.Model.extend({
  validation: {
    terms: {
      acceptance: true
    },
  }
});
```

- **min**: It validates that the attribute value has to be a number and equal to or greater than the min value specified.

```
var BuyerModel = Backbone.Model.extend({
  validation: {
    age: {
      min: 18
    },
  }
});
```

- **max**: It validates that the attribute value has to be a number and equal to or less than the max value specified.

```
var EventRegistrationModel = Backbone.Model.extend({
  validation: {
    guests: {
      max: 2
    },
  }
});
```

- **range**: It validates that the attribute value has to be a number and equal to or between the two numbers specified.

```
var ChildTicketModel = Backbone.Model.extend({
  validation: {
    age: {
      range: [2, 12]
    },
  }
});
```

- **length**: It validates that the attribute value has to be a string with length equal to the length value specified.

```
var AddressModel = Backbone.Model.extend({
  validation: {
    zip: {
      length: 5
    },
  }
});
```

- **minLength**: It validates that the attribute value has to be a string with length equal to or greater than the min length value specified.

```
var UserModel = Backbone.Model.extend({
  validation: {
```

```
       password: {
         minLength: 8
       },
     }
   });
```

▶ **maxLength**: It validates that the attribute value has to be a string with length equal to or less than the max length value specified.

```
var UserModel = Backbone.Model.extend({
  validation: {
    password: {
      maxLength: 8
    },
  }
});
```

▶ **rangeLength**: It validates that the attribute value has to be a string and equal to or between the two numbers specified.

```
var BuyerModel = Backbone.Model.extend({
  validation: {
    phoneNumber: {
      rangeLength: [10, 12]
    },
  }
});
```

▶ **oneOf**: It validates that the attribute value has to be equal to one of the elements in the specified array. It uses case-sensitive matching.

```
var BuyerModel = Backbone.Model.extend({
  validation: {
    type: {
      oneOf: [''person'', ''organization'']
    },
  }
});
```

▶ **equalTo**: It validates that the attribute value has to be equal to the value of the attribute with the name specified.

```
var UserModel = Backbone.Model.extend({
  validation: {
    password: {
      required: true
    },
    passwordRepeat: {
```

```
        equalTo: 'password'
      }
    }
  });
```

▶ **pattern**: It validates that the attribute value has to match the pattern specified. It can be a regular expression or the name of one of the built-in patterns.

```
var BuyerModel = Backbone.Model.extend({
  validation: {
    email: {
      pattern: 'email'
    }
  }
});
```

Pattern can accept one of the following attribute values:

- ❑ **number**: matches any decimal number
- ❑ **digits**: matches any digit sequence
- ❑ **email**: matches a valid email address
- ❑ **url**: matches any valid URL

You can also specify any regular expression instead.

```
var BuyerModel = Backbone.Model.extend({
  validation: {
    phoneNumber: {
      pattern: /^(\+\d)*\s*(\(\d{3}\)\s*)*\d{3}(-
        {0,1}|\s{0,1})\d{2}(-{0,1}|\s{0,1})\d{2}$/
    }
  }
});
```

See also

▶ In this recipe, we learned the basics of the `Backbone.Validation` extension, though there are even more techniques that you can find on the **GitHub** documentation page `https://github.com/thedersen/backbone.validation`.

▶ There are also a couple of alternatives to `Backbone.Validation`. They are `Backbone.validations` and `Backbone.Validator` extensions. They are all very similar, but `Backbone.Validation` has better documentation and provides more methods and events.

Validating an HTML form

Most of the web applications use HTML forms for data input, and Backbone is not an exception. An application should let the user know about any validation errors. Implementation of such functionality could fall on the developers' shoulders, but not in Backbone!

Fortunately, `Backbone.Validation` provides integration with a view and works well with HTML forms.

Getting ready

Make sure you have the `Backbone.Validation` extension installed. Installation is described in the previous recipe *Using advanced validation in a model*.

How to do it...

Perform the following step to validate a form:

To allow form validation, we need to bind a view to a `Backbone.Validation` object in the `initialize()` method of the view.

```
Backbone.Validation.bind(this);
```

`Backbone.Validation` assumes that your model is stored in `this.model` and you have implemented getting data from the form elements and updating model values with it.

How it works...

If a user enters information that does not validate, then `Backbone.Validation` adds the `invalid` class to an appropriate form element and sets the `data-error` attribute with an error message.

> `data-*` attributes are an HTML5 feature. They can be easily displayed with the help of CSS3 or custom JavaScript. They are also supported by major web frontend frameworks, such as jQueryMobile or Twitter Bootstrap.

The following screenshot illustrates how `Backbone.Validation` validates wrong data entered into the HTML form:

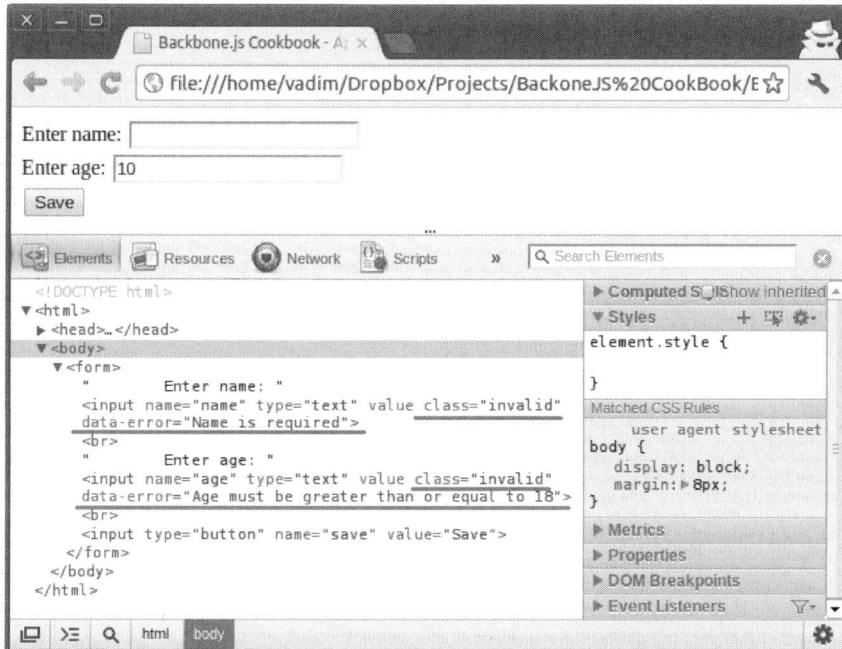

There's more...

The following code snippet is a full listing of the example for this recipe:

```
(function($){

  // Define new model.
  var BuyerModel = Backbone.Model.extend({
    defaults: {
      name: '',
      age: ''
    },

    // Define validation criteria.
    validation: {
      name: {
        required: true
      },
      age: {
        min: 18
      }
    }
```

```javascript
});

var BuyerModelFormView = Backbone.View.extend({

  // Bind Backbone.Validation to a view.
  initialize: function(){
    Backbone.Validation.bind(this);
  },

  // Define a template.
  template: _.template('\
    <form>\
      Enter name:\
      <input name="name" type="text" value="<%= name %>"><br>\
      Enter age:\
      <input name="age" type="text" value="<%= age %>"><br>\
      <input type="button" name="save" value="Save">\
    </form>\
  '),

  // Render view.
  render: function(){
    // Render template with model values.
    var html = this.template(this.model.toJSON());

    // Update html.
    $(this.el).html(html);
  },

  // Bind save callback click event.
  events: {
    'click [name~="save"]': 'save'
  },

  // Save callback.
  save: function(){

    // Update model attributes.
    this.model.set({
      name: $('[name~="name"]').val(),
      age: $('[name~="age"]').val()
    });
  }
});
```

```
$(document).ready(function () {
    // Create new model instance.
    var buyerModel = new BuyerModel();

    // Create new view instance.
    var buyerModelFormView = new BuyerModelFormView({
        model: buyerModel,
        el: 'body'
    });

    // Render view.
    buyerModelFormView.render();
});
})(jQuery);
```

Working with nested attributes in a model

Sometimes nested attributes are required to operate with complex hierarchical structures stored in the model. This is typically done by using JavaScript objects as nested attributes; however, it is not a Backbone way. Fortunately, there is the `Backbone-Nested` extension, which provides various improvements when working with nested attributes.

Getting ready

You can download the `Backbone-Nested` extension from the **GitHub** page `https://github.com/afeld/backbone-nested`. To include this extension into your project, save the `backbone-nested.js` file into the `lib` folder and include a reference to it in `index.html`.

> Including Backbone extension into your project is described in the *Extending application with plugins* recipe in *Chapter 1, Understanding Backbone* in detail.

How to do it...

Perform the following steps to use nested attributes in a model:

1. Use `Backnone.NestedModel` as the base object when extending a new model.

   ```
   var BuyerModel = Backbone.NestedModel.extend({

   });
   ```

2. Set the nested attribute value with the help of dot syntax provided by the `Backbone-Nested` extension.

```
buyerModel.set({
    'name.title': 'Mr',
    'name.generation': 'II'
});
```

You can still use object syntax, which is typical to JavaScript, to set multiple values.

```
buyerModel.set({
    name: {
        first: 'John',
        last: 'Smith',
        middle: {
            initial: 'P',
            full: 'Peter'
        }
    }
});
```

3. Get the attribute value with the dot syntax.

```
buyerModel.get('name.middle.full'); // Peter
buyerModel.get('name.middle');
// { full: 'Peter', initial: 'P' }
buyerModel.get('name.title'); // Mr
```

How it works...

The `Backbone-Nested` extension provides a new model object `Backbone.NestedModel` based on `Backbone.Model`. It overrides existing methods, such as `get()`, `set()`, `has()`, `toJSON`, and so on. It also provides new `add()` and `remove()` methods.

There's more...

This section describes advanced usage of the `Backbone-Nested` extension.

Working with a nested array of attributes

Of course, there is a way of working with a bit more complex structures, such as nested array of attributes. You can set it using the object syntax as well.

```
buyerModel.set({
    'addresses': [
        {city: 'Brooklyn', state: 'NY'},
```

```
    {city: 'Oak Park', state: 'IL'}
  ]
});
```

Or you can set attributes in the nested array with a dot and bracket syntax, as shown in following example:

```
buyerModel.set({
  'addresses[1].state': 'MI'
});
```

And the same syntax is used for getting attributes from the nested array.

```
buyerModel.get('addresses[0].state'); // NY
buyerModel.get('addresses[1].state'); // MI
```

Adding/removing elements to/from a nested array

`Backbone-Nested` provides additional methods to work with nested arrays. The `add` method adds a new element to a nested array. Here is how it works.

```
buyerModel.add('addresses', {
  city: 'Seattle',
  state: 'WA'
});

buyerModel.get('addresses[2]');
// { city: 'Seattle', state: 'WA' }
```

The `remove()` method removes desired elements from a nested array. Let's see how it is done.

```
buyerModel.remove('addresses[1]');

buyerModel.get('addresses').length; // 2
```

Binding callbacks to an events

When binding a callback to an event, you can use the same dot and bracket syntax as described previously. Let's check out the following example of binding a callback to an event:

```
buyerModel.bind('change:addresses[0].city', function(model, value){
  console.log(value);
});

buyerModel.set('addresses[0].city', 'Chicago');
```

Moreover, `Backbone-Nested` provides additional `add:*` and `remove:*` events for handling array update events.

▶ There is more information about event handling available in the recipe *Handling events of Backbone objects* in *Chapter 5, Events and Bindings*.

▶ There are a couple of alternatives to the `Backbone-Nested` extension, such as `Backbone-deep-model` and `Backbone-dotattr`. They are all very similar, but `Backbone-Nested` provides more features, and is better maintained.

Implementing a one-to-one relationship

Mostly in any application, we may need to have models that are related to each other. For example, a blog post model can have a relationship with a model of its author or have a connection to a comment model.

We may also need to access comments quickly when dealing with a blog post, or list all blog posts of a specific author. Moreover, we may want to export blog posts with author info and comments in a single JSON format.

In a Backbone app, this can be implemented with the help of the `Backbone-relational` extension.

Getting ready

You can download the `Backbone-relational` extension from the **GitHub** page `https://github.com/PaulUithol/Backbone-relational`. To include `Backbone-relational` into your project, save the `backbone-relational.js` file into the `lib` folder and include a reference to it in `index.html`.

> Including a Backbone extension into your project is described in the *Extending application with plugins* recipe in *Chapter 1, Understanding Backbone* in detail.

How to do it...

Let's recall our Invoice application and try to find out how we can apply a one-to-one relationship there. Let's say we want buyers to log in to the application and view all invoices assigned to them.

In this case, we need to store buyer credentials somewhere. It can be a new `UserModel` associated with an existing `BuyerModel`. We know that for each user there is a single buyer and vice versa, so we are dealing with a one-to-one relationship. Let's implement one such one-to-one relationship.

1. Extend models from `Backbone.RelationalModel` and pass the `relations` property with a relationship definition.

```
// Define new model object.
var UserModel = Backbone.RelationalModel.extend({

});

// Define new model object.
var BuyerModel = Backbone.RelationalModel.extend({

  // Define one-to-one relationship.
  relations: [
    {
      // Relationship type
      type: Backbone.HasOne,

      // Relationship key in BuyerModel.
      key: 'user',

      // Related model.
      relatedModel: UserModel,

      // Define reverse relationship.
      reverseRelation: {
        type: Backbone.HasOne,
        key: 'buyer'
      }
    }
  ]
});
```

As we see from the previous example, the `relations` property takes an array, so multiple relationships are possible.

> Note that `UserModel` should be defined before `BuyerModel`, because it is referenced afterwards in the code (in the `relations` property of BuyerModel).

2. Initialize a one-to-one relationship by referencing the `UserModel` instance in the `BuyerModel` instance or vice versa.

```
var userModel1 = new UserModel({
  login: 'jsmith',
  email: 'jsmith@example.com'
```

```
  });

  var buyerModel1 = new BuyerModel({
    firstName: 'John',
    lastName: 'Smith',
    user: userModel1
  });
```

There is also a way to do the same by passing a single input JSON when creating both `BuyerModel` and `UserModel`.

```
  var buyerModel = new BuyerModel({
    firstName: 'John',
    lastName: 'Smith',
    user: {
      login: 'jsmith',
      email: 'jsmith@example.com'
    }
  });
```

3. If a reversed relation is defined, pass a `BuyerModel` array when initializing `UserModel`.

```
  var userModel = new UserModel({
    login: 'jsmith',
    email: 'jsmith@example.com',
    buyer: {
      firstName: 'John',
      lastName: 'Smith'
    }
  });
```

4. Optionally, access the related model with the help of the `get()` method.

```
  buyerModel1.get('user').get('email');
  // jsmith@example.com
  userModel1.get('buyer').get('lastName'); // Smith
```

How it works...

Each `Backbone.RelationalModel` registers itself with `Backbone.Store` upon creation (and is removed from the `Store` when destroyed). When creating or updating an attribute that is a key in a relation, removed related objects are notified of their removal, and new related objects are looked up in the `Store`.

See also

► One-to-many relationships and many-to-many relationships are described in the recipe *Implementing a one-to-many relationship* in *Chapter 3, Collections*.

► Complete documentation to the `Backbone-relational` extension can be found on the **GitHub** page `https://github.com/PaulUithol/Backbone-relational`.

► Also, there are a couple of alternatives to `Backbone-relational`, which are very similar and known as `Backbone-associations` and `ligament.js`. However, they do not provide one-to-many and many-to-many relationships.

3
Collections

In this chapter we will cover:

- ▸ Creating a collection of models
- ▸ Getting a model from a collection by its index
- ▸ Getting a model from a collection by its ID
- ▸ Adding a model to a collection
- ▸ Removing a model from a collection
- ▸ Working with a collection as a stack or as a queue
- ▸ Sorting a collection
- ▸ Filtering models in a collection
- ▸ Iterating through a collection
- ▸ Chaining a collection
- ▸ Running No SQL queries on a collection
- ▸ Storing models of various types in the same collection
- ▸ Implementing a one-to-many relationship

Introduction

When developing applications with Backbone, you often need to work with a number of models, which can be organized in a collection. A collection is more than just a JavaScript array. Backbone provides various useful methods to work with it. Moreover, Backbone collection can easily communicate with a REST server to get or post a number of models.

In this chapter, we are going to learn common operations to work with collections, and will discover new extensions which provide amazing functionality.

Creating a collection of models

In this recipe, we are going to learn how to create a collection of models. Collection is an object used for organizing models into an ordered set. There are specific methods to sort, filter, and iterate through a collection.

How to do it...

Follow these steps to create a collection:

1. Extend the `Backbone.Collection` object and pass the model's object name as an option.

```
var InvoiceItemCollection = Backbone.Collection.extend
({
    model: InvoiceItemModel
});
```

2. Initialize a new collection instance and pass the initial array of models.

```
var invoiceItemCollection = new InvoiceItemCollection
([
    {description: 'Wooden Toy House', price: 22, quantity: 3},
    {description: 'Farm Animal Set', price: 17, quantity: 1},
    {description: 'Farmer Figure', price: 8, quantity: 1},
    {description: 'Toy Tractor', price: 15, quantity: 1}
]);
```

How it works...

`Backbone.Collection` knows which model object to use when creating new instances, because we specified it in the `model` property. Internally, models are stored in the `models` array.

There's more...

We can also initialize a collection with the existing models. Here is how it is done.

```
invoiceItemModel1 = new InvoiceItemModel
({
    description: 'Wooden Toy House',
    price: 22,
```

```
      quantity: 3
    });
invoiceItemModel2 = new InvoiceItemModel
    ({
       description: 'Farm Animal Set',
       price: 17,
       quantity: 1
    });
var invoiceItemCollection2 = new InvoiceItemCollection
    ([
       invoiceItemModel1,
       invoiceItemModel2
    ]);
```

Getting a model from a collection by its index

When working with a collection, we may need to get a model at the specific index, because it is stored inside the collection.

How to do it...

Use the `at()` method to get a model from a collection at the specific index.

```
var model = invoiceItemCollection.at(2);
model.get('description'); // Farmer Figure
```

How it works...

Internally, models are stored in the `models` array, so the first element starts with a zero index. `Backbone.Collection` keeps this array in the accurate state when we add a new model to a collection, remove one model, or perform sorting.

> **Be careful when sorting a collection**
>
> When performing a collection, sorting it can update the model indexes, so the `at()` method with the same parameter can get different models before and after sorting.

There's more...

In this section, we are going to learn some interesting details about models in a collection.

Getting an index of a collection model

To get an index of a model stored in a collection, use the `indexOf()` method inherited from `Underscore.js`.

```
invoiceItemCollection.indexOf(model); // 2
```

Getting an independent copy of a model

The model object that is retrieved from a collection is the same object stored there, so if we modify this object, one object in the collection gets updated.

```
model.set('description', 'Superman Figure');
invoiceItemCollection.at(2).get('description');
// Superman Figure
```

If we need to get an independent copy of the model object, we can use the `clone()` method of a returned model. Changing the attributes of the cloned model does not affect the attributes of the original model.

```
var anotherModel = invoiceItemCollection.at(2).clone();
anotherModel.set('description', 'Another Figure');
invoiceItemCollection.at(2).get('description');
// Superman Figure
```

Getting the length of a collection

There is a way to get the length of a collection. It is done with the help of the `length()` method. The following example gets a collection length and then obtains the last model from the collection:

```
var length = invoiceItemCollection.length; //4
model = invoiceItemCollection.at(length-1);
model.get('description'); // Toy Tractor
```

Getting a model from a collection by its ID

In our application, we may need to request a model from a collection by its ID.

How to do it...

Follow these steps to get a model from a collection by its ID:

1. To get a model from a collection by its identifier, use the `get()` method.

```
model = invoiceItemCollection2.get('4ryurtz3m5gn9udi');
```

2. To get a model from a collection by its client identifier, you can again use the `get()` method.

```
model = invoiceItemCollection.get('c4');
model.get('description'); // Toy Tractor
```

How it works...

When getting a model by its ID, `Backbone.Collection` searches for the model in the `_byId` array, which stores models mapped to their IDs. Such an implementation guarantees the best performance, because there is no need to loop through all the models in a collection.

See also

▸ *Extending an application with plugins* in *Chapter 2, Models*

Adding a model to a collection

In this recipe, we are going to learn different ways of adding new models to a collection.

How to do it...

Call the `add()` method to add a new model to the end of a collection.

```
invoiceItemCollection.add
  ({
    description: 'Toy Track',
    price: 10,
    quantity: 1
  });
```

How it works...

The code in the add() method prevents duplicates from being added to the collection. A unique model is inserted into the models array and is mapped to its ID in the _byId array. Also, a reference to the collection is created in the model object in the collection property.

By default, a new model is added to the end of the collection. But in case sorting is enabled, or insertion index is specified, the model can be inserted at a different position.

When adding a new model to a collection, the add event is being triggered.

There's more...

In this section, we are going to learn different ways to add a model(s) into a collection.

Adding a model at a specific position

To add a model at a specific position, we need to pass {at: index} as an option.

```
invoiceItemCollection.add
  (
    {description: 'Fisherman Hut', price: 15, quantity: 1},
    {at: 0}
  );
invoiceItemCollection.at(0).get('description');
// Fisherman Hut
```

Adding multiple models

We can also add multiple models at the same time.

```
invoiceItemCollection.add
  ([
    {description: 'Powerboat', price: 12, quantity: 1},
    {description: 'Jet Ski', price: 12, quantity: 1}
  ]);
```

Adding existing models

We can also use existing model objects as the arguments for the add() method. We can pass a single object as well as an array of existing objects.

See also

▸ *Handling events of Backbone objects* in *Chapter 5, Events and Bindings*

Removing a model from a collection

In this recipe, we are going to learn about removing a model from a collection.

How to do it...

Call the `remove()` method to remove a model from a collection.

```
invoiceItemCollection.remove(['c0', 'c1', 'c2', 'c3']);
```

Here we can pass the model's `id`, `cid`, or even the model object as a parameter. We can either pass a single value or an array of values.

How it works...

When calling the `remove()` method, a model is removed from the `models` array, and any references between them are removed as well. Thus, the model object itself is not destroyed, and we can still work with it if the need arises.

There's more...

Sometimes, we may need to delete all the existing models from a collection and add some others. There is a useful `reset()` method, which does both these jobs simultaneously. Here is how it works.

```
invoiceItemCollection.reset   ([
    {description: 'Wooden Toy House', price: 22, quantity: 3},
    {description: 'Farm Animal Set', price: 17, quantity: 1}
]);
```

Working with a collection as a stack or as a queue

There are special methods in Backbone that allow working with a collection as a stack or as a queue.

How to do it...

Follow these steps to work with a collection as a stack or as a queue:

1. Call the `push()` method to add a model to the end of a collection.

    ```
    invoiceItemCollection.push(model);
    ```

2. Call the `pop()` method to remove and return the last model from a collection.

    ```
    model = invoiceItemCollection.pop();
    ```

3. Call the `unshift()` method to add a model at the beginning of a collection.

    ```
    invoiceItemCollection.unshift(model);
    ```

4. Call the `shift()` method to remove and return the first model from a collection.

    ```
    model = invoiceItemCollection.shift();
    ```

How it works...

To organize a stack also known as LIFO (last in, first out), we need to use the `push` and `pop` (`unshift` and `shift`) methods. To organize a queue also known as FIFO (first in, first out), we need to use the `unshift` and `pop` (`push` and `shift`) methods.

The following image illustrates the difference between a stack and a queue:

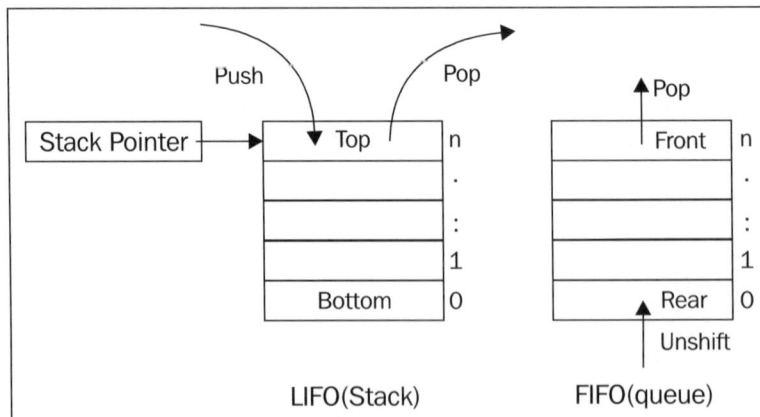

Sorting a collection

`Backbone.js` provides a sorting mechanism, out of the box, which we are going to learn in this recipe.

How to do it...

Follow these steps to sort a collection:

1. Assign the `comparator` callback to the `comparator` property of a collection to maintain the correct order.

   ```
   invoiceItemCollection.comparator = function(model)
     {
       return model.get("price");
     };
   ```

2. The `comparator` callback accepts a single parameter, which is a model object. It should return a value according to which the collection is sorted.

3. Optionally, call the `sort()` method to force sorting.

   ```
   invoiceItemCollection.sort();
   ```

4. Check the result.

   ```
   invoiceItemCollection.pluck("price"); // [8, 15, 17, 22]
   ```

How it works...

When the `comparator` callback is defined, Backbone uses it to insert a new model in the `models` array so that it is inserted in the correct order.

If you assign a new `comparator` callback to a collection with existing models, you need to trigger sorting manually by calling the `sort()` method.

You also need to call the `sort()` method if the model in the collection gets updated. This can be done automatically if you bind sorting on the model's `change` event.

There's more...

In this section, we are going to define a comparator in a different way.

Comparing a pair of models in the comparator

Another way to implement a comparator is to evaluate a pair of models passed as parameters and return one of the following values:

- ▶ -1 (or any negative value), if the first model should come before the second
- ▶ 0, if they are of the same rank
- ▶ 1 (or any positive value), if the first model should come after the second

The following example demonstrates sorting by the length of the `description` attribute:

```
invoiceItemCollection.comparator = function(m1, m1)
  {
    return m1.get("description").length -
    m2.get("description").length;
  };
invoiceItemCollection.sort();
invoiceItemCollection.pluck("description");
// ["Toy Tractor", "Farmer Figure", "Farm Animal Set",
// "Wooden Toy
```

See also

- ▶ *Handling events of Backbone objects* in *Chapter 5, Events and Bindings*

Filtering models in a collection

Backbone provides a simple filtering mechanism out of the box, which we can use.

How to do it...

To filter models in a collection, use the `where()` method. It accepts a search criteria and returns an array of found models.

```
var result = invoiceItemCollection.where({quantity: 1});
// Result is just an array of models, so let's create
// new collection.
var resultCollection = new InvoiceItemCollection(result);
resultCollection.pluck('quantity'); // [1, 1, 1]
```

It is also possible to pass multiple criteria together.

```
invoiceItemCollection.where({quantity: 1, price: 10});
```

See also

▶ Refer to the *Running No SQL queries on a collection* recipe to learn more about advanced filtering

Iterating through a collection

In this recipe, we are going to discuss various ways of iterating through a collection to implement the functionality we need.

How to do it...

The easiest way to iterate through a collection is to use the `each()` method provided by `Underscore.js`.

```
var  descriptions_txt = '';
invoiceItemCollection.each(function(model, index, list)
  {
     descriptions_txt += descriptions_txt ? ', ' : '';
     descriptions_txt += model.get('description');
  });
descriptions_txt; // Wooden Toy House, Farm Animal Set
```

In the `each()` method, we pass an iterator function, which is executed for each model. It accepts the following parameters:

▶ **model**: The model that is being iterated

▶ **index**: This is the model index

▶ **list**: This is the whole model array

How it works...

`Backbone.js` is based on `Underscore.js`, which provides various useful tools, including methods to work with the collections and arrays. Backbone collections support some of those functions.

There's more...

In this section, we are going to learn some methods that rely on the iteration method but are more specific.

Checking every model to match a specific condition

To check every model in a collection that fulfills a specific criteria, use the `every()` method. It accepts a callback parameter which should return a `Boolean` value if the condition is fulfilled.

```
var multiple = invoiceItemCollection.every(function(model)
  {
    return model.get('quantity') > 1;
  });
multiple; // false
```

Checking any model to match a specific condition

To check any model in a collection that fulfills a specific criteria, use the `some()` method. It accepts a callback parameter which should return a `Boolean` value if the condition is fulfilled.

```
var multiple = invoiceItemCollection.some(function(model)
  {
    return model.get('quantity') > 1;
});
multiple; // true
```

Getting the attribute from each model in a collection

In the previous examples, we used the `pluck()` method, which returns an array of values for the specified attribute from each model in a collection. Let's see how it works.

```
var descriptions = invoiceItemCollection.pluck("description");
descriptions; // ["Wooden Toy House", "Farm Animal Set"]
```

Performing specific calculations to each model in a collection

To perform specific calculations to each model in a collection, use the `map()` method. It takes callback as a parameter, executes it for each model in a collection, and returns an array of results.

```
var amounts = invoiceItemCollection.map(function(model)
  {
    return model.get('quantity') * model.get('price');
  });
amounts; // [66, 77]
```

Boiling down models in a collection into a single value

Models in a collection can be boiled down to a single value using the `reduce()` method.
Here is how it works.

```
var count = invoiceItemCollection.reduce(function(memo,model)
  {
    return memo + model.get('quantity');
  }, 0);
count; // 4
```

See also

> ▸   There are many helpful methods from `Underscore.js` that can be used with
>   Backbone collections. You can find them in `Underscore.js` official docs from
>   `http://documentcloud.github.com/underscore/#collections`.

Chaining a collection

If you want to perform several Underscore methods in a row, a good way of doing it is by
chaining one method to the other method.

Let's consider a simple MapReduce example, which calculates the total amount.

```
var amounts = invoiceItemCollection.map(function(model)
  {
    return model.get('quantity') * model.get('price');
  });
// [66, 77]
var total_amount = _.reduce(amounts, function(memo, val)
  {
    return memo + val;
  }, 0);
total_amount; // 83
```

Here, `amounts` is a JavaScript array, and it does not provide the `reduce()` method that we can
call. To solve this problem, we are calling the `reduce()` method provided by `Underscore.js`,
which takes an array as the first parameter.

How to do it...

With chaining, it is possible to call one method right after another using the `dot` syntax. Here is an example.

```
var amount = invoiceItemCollection.chain()
.map(function(model)
  {
    return model.get('quantity') * model.get('price');
  })
.reduce(function(memo, val)
  {
    return memo + val;
  })
.value(); // 83
```

How it works...

The `chain()` method wraps a value into an object, which provides different methods that can be executed, which return their result as a wrapped value. To unwrap a result, use the `value()` method.

See also

▶ To see more chaining examples, please visit `http://documentcloud.github.com/underscore/#chain`

Running No SQL queries on a collection

In the previous recipe we described several techniques, including the one about searching the models in a collection with the `where()` method.

There are more advanced ways of searching the models in a collection, which can be done with the help of a Backbone extension named **Backbone Query**. It allows running No SQL (such as MongoDB) queries for searching, sorting, and paging the models in a collection.

Getting ready

You can download the Backbone Query extension from its GitHub page by going to `https://github.com/davidgtonge/backbone_query`. To include this extension into your project, save the `backbone-query.js` file into the `lib` folder and include the reference to it in `index.html`.

> Including the Backbone extension into your project is described in detail in the *Extending an application with plugins* recipe in *Chapter 1, Understanding Backbone*.

How to do it...

Follow these steps to perform a No SQL query to a collection:

1. To allow a No SQL query to be executed, extend a collection from the `Backbone.QueryCollection` object instead of a `Backbone.Collection` one.

```
var BuyerCollection = Backbone.QueryCollection.extend
   ({
      model: BuyerModel
   });
```

2. Run the query with the `query()` method.

```
var result = buyerCollection.query({ firstName: 'John' });
```

3. Optionally, run the `pluck` attribute from the resulting array.

```
var resultCollection = new BuyerCollection(result);
resultCollection.pluck('firstName'); // ["John", "John"]
```

How it works...

`Backbone.QueryCollection` extends `Backbone.Collection` and provides the new `query()` method, which parses the base query into subqueries recursively and uses the `reduce()` method of `Underscore.js` to run queries of the same group sequentially.

Backbone Query is written initially in CoffeeScript and compiled into JavaScript later. So, if you are interested in understanding its source code, see `backbone-query.coffee`. It looks quite similar though.

There's more...

This section describes No SQL operators and covers some advanced topics, such as grouping, sorting, paging, and caching.

Using standard operators

The following operators are common and applied to the attributes of the models stored in a collection.

$equal

This performs a strict equality test using `===`.

```
buyerCollection.query({ firstName: {$equal: 'John'} });
```

If no operator is provided, and the query value is neither a regex nor an array, then `$equal` is assumed.

```
buyerCollection.query({ firstName: 'John' });
```

$ne

This means not equal, which is the opposite of `$equal`, and returns all the models that are not equal to the query value.

```
buyerCollection.query({ firstName: {$ne: 'John'} });
```

$in

An array of possible values can be supplied using `$in`; a model will be returned if any of the supplied values is matched.

```
buyerCollection.query({ firstName: {$in: ['John', 'Joe',
    'Patrick']} });
```

$nin

This means not in, which is the opposite of `$in`, and a model will be returned if none of the supplied values is matched.

```
buyerCollection.query
({ firstName: {$nin: ['Samuel', 'Victor']} });
```

$exists or $has

This checks for the existence of an attribute, and can be supplied as either `true` or `false`.

```
buyerCollection.query({ middleName: {$exists: true} });
```

```
buyerCollection.query({ middleName: {$has: false} });
```

Combining queries

Multiple queries can be combined together. There are the `$and`, `$or`, `$nor`, and `$not` operators, which we are going to learn shortly.

$and

This is a logical AND operator. The following query selects all the buyers named John and who live in Alexandria:

```
buyerCollection.query
   ({ $and: {firstName: 'John', city: 'Alexandria'}});
```

The $and operator is used as a glue if no combining operator is supplied.

```
buyerCollection.query
   ({ firstName: 'John', city: 'Alexandria' });
```

$or

This is a logical OR operator. The following query selects all the buyers named John or whether the buyers live in Alexandria:

```
buyerCollection.query
   ({ $or: {firstName: 'John', city: 'Alexandria'}});
```

$nor

This is the opposite of $or. The following query selects all the buyers with a name other than John or if they do not live in Alexandria:

```
buyerCollection.query
   ({ $nor: {firstName: 'John', city: 'Alexandria'}});
```

$not

This is the opposite of $and. The following query selects all buyers except anyone whose name is John and who lives in Alexandria:

```
buyerCollection.query
   ({ $not: {firstName: 'John', city: 'Alexandria'}});
```

Multiple queries on the same key

If we need to perform multiple queries on the same key, then we can supply the query as an array. The following query returns all the clients with the name John or Joe:

```
buyerCollection.query
   ({
     $or: [
       { firstName: 'John' },
       { firstName: 'Joe' }
     ]
   });
```

Sorting query results

To sort results by a property, we need to pass it with the `sortBy` key in a second argument. We can also specify the order by passing the `asc` or `desc` value with the `sort` key. By default, `asc` is assumed as the value. The following code shows how sorting is done:

```
result = buyerCollection.query
    (
        { firstName: {$like: 'John'} },
        { sortBy: 'lastName', order: 'desc' }
    );
resultCollection = new BuyerCollection(result);
resultCollection.pluck('lastName'); // ["Smith", "Doe"]
```

Paging query results

There is a way to split a big result array on several pages and return a specified one. Let's see how it is done.

```
buyerCollection.query
({firstName: 'John'}, {limit:10, offset:1, page:2});
```

We can specify the following properties in the second parameter:

- ▶ `limit`: It limits the resulting array size to a given number. The first N elements are returned. It is a required property.
- ▶ `page`: It returns a specified resulting page. The page size is set by the limit property. It is an optional property.
- ▶ `offset`: It skips the first N result items. It is an optional property.

Caching results

For performance reasons, we may want to cache our results. This can greatly decrease the query execution time, especially if using paging, because unpaged results are saved in the cache and a user can quickly navigate through its pages.

To enable caching, simply use the `cache` property in the second parameter.

```
buyerCollection.query
({firstName: 'John'}, {limit:10, page:2, cache: true});
```

Caching is not set by default, because there is no automatic way to flush the cache, so when caching is enabled and the collection is being updated, the cache becomes outdated.

You should be aware of this problem, and manually perform cache flushing every time the collections or models in it are updated. This can be done by calling the `reset_query_cache()` method.

We can bind the collection's `change` event to the `reset_query_cache()` method, and thus, provide automatic cache flushing when the collection gets updated.

```
var BuyerCollection = Backbone.QueryCollection.extend
({
    initialize: function(){
        this.bind('change', this.reset_query_cache, this);
    }
});
```

See also

▸ Please see more information about Backbone query operators from https://github.com/davidgtonge/backbone_query#query-api

▸ *Handling events of Backbone objects* in *Chapter 5, Events and Bindings*

Storing models of various types in the same collection

When building complex Backbone applications, you may need to work with models of different types, which should be processed in a similar way, so you may want them to be stored in the same collection. Fortunately, there is a `Backbone.Chosen` extension that allow us to do so.

Getting ready

You can find and download `Backbone.Chosen` from the following page: `https://github.com/asciidisco/Backbone.Chosen`. To include `Backbone.Chosen` into your project, save the `backbone.chosen.js` file into the `lib` folder and include the reference to it in `index.html`.

> Including Backbone extension into your project is described in detail in the *Extending an application with plugins* recipe in *Chapter 1, Understanding Backbone*.

How to do it...

Let's say we have two different model classes, namely `IndividualContactModel` and `OrganizationContactModel`, and we want to organize them into a single collection. We can do this by performing the following steps:

1. Define models.

```
var IndividualContactModel = Backbone.Model.extend
  ({
    name: function() {
      return this.get('firstName') + ' ' + this.get('lastName');
    }
  });

var OrganizationContactModel = Backbone.Model.extend
  ({
    name: function() {
      return this.get('businessName') + ', '
      + this.get('businessType');
    }
  });
```

As we can see, these models have different attributes, but share a common `name()` method.

2. Define collection with a `chosen` attribute.

```
var ContactCollection = Backbone.Collection.extend
  ({
    model: {
      // Pass chosen properties.
      chosen: {
          // Attribute that should contain model type.
          attr: 'type',

          // Default model class.
          defaults: IndividualContactModel,

          // Mapping attribute values to model classes.
          map: {
            individual: IndividualContactModel,
            organization: OrganizationContactModel
          }
        }
      }
  });
```

3. Create a collection instance and specify the mapping attribute in the incoming JSON.

```
var contactCollection = new ContactCollection
  ([
    {
      firstName: 'John',
      lastName: 'Smith',
      type: 'individual'
    },
    {
      businessName: 'North American Veeblefetzer',
      businessType: 'LLC',
      type: 'organization'
    }
  ]);
```

4. Check the result. The newly added models to the collection should be the instance of the correct model class.

```
contactCollection.at(0) instanceof IndividualContactModel;
//true

contactCollection.at(0).name(); // John Smith

contactCollection.at(1) instanceof OrganizationContactModel;
//true

contactCollection.at(1).name();
// North American Veeblefetzer, LLC
```

How it works...

`Backbone.Chosen` overrides the `_prepareModel` method of `Backbone.Collection` to select the proper model object that depends on its mapping attribute value.

There's more...

This section explains how to perform advanced mapping.

Mapping deeply nested attributes

`Backbone.Chosen` also supports nested attributes. You can specify the value for the `attr` property with a `dot` syntax, for example, `options.type`, if your incoming JSON looks like the following code:

```
var contactCollection = new ContactCollection
  ([
```

```
      {
        firstName: 'John',
        lastName: 'Smith',
        options: {type: 'individual'}
      },
      {
        businessName: 'North American Veeblefetzer',
        businessType: 'LLC',
        options: {type: 'organization'}
      }
    ]);
```

Use a function to map the models

Sometimes, we may need to use more complex calculations to map the models. This can be done with the help of the mapping function. Here is how it is done.

```
// Set up a collection
var ContactCollection = Backbone.Collection.extend({
  model: {
    chosen: function (rawData) {
      if (rawData.spice === 'salt') {
        return SaltyModel;
        }
      if (rawData.spice === 'sugar') {
        return SweetyModel;
        }
      return BoringModel;
      }
    }
  });
```

Implementing a one-to-many relationship

In *Chapter 2, Models*, there is a recipe about creating a one-to-one relationship between two models. In this recipe, we are going to learn about creating one-to-many relationships.

A one-to-many relationship can be used if the association between a single model and a collection of models of another type takes place. In our invoice application, the relationship between `InvoiceModel` and `InvoiceItemModel` is one such relationship. InvoiceItem Model can be multiple and thus is stored in `InvoiceItemCollection`.

Getting ready

You can download the Backbone-relational extension from its GitHub page at `https://github.com/PaulUithol/Backbone-relational`. To include `Backbone.Relational` into your project, save the `backbone-relational.js` file into the `lib` folder and include the reference to it in `index.html`.

> Including Backbone extension into your project is described in detail in the *Extending an application with plugins* recipe in *Chapter 1, Understanding Backbone*.

How to do it...

Implementation of a one-to-many relationship is similar to an implementation of a one-to-one relationship, except that we need to use `Backbone.HasMany` as a type and specify `collectionType`, because multiple models should be stored in the collection. We can do this by performing the following steps:

1. Extend the new model object from `Backbone.RelationalModel`.

```
var InvoiceItemModel = Backbone.RelationalModel.extend
  ({
  });
```

2. Define the collection for this model type.

```
var InvoiceItemCollection = Backbone.Collection.extend
  ({
    model: InvoiceItemModel
  });
```

3. Extend another model object from `Backbone.RelationalModel` and pass the `relations` property with a relationship definition.

```
var InvoiceModel = Backbone.RelationalModel.extend
  ({
    // Define one-to-many relationship.
    relations: [{
      // Relationship type
      type: Backbone.HasMany,

      // Relationship key in BuyerModel.
      key: 'items',
```

```
  // Related model.
  relatedModel: InvoiceItemModel,

  // Collection to store related models.
  collectionType: InvoiceItemCollection,

  // Define reverse relationship.
  reverseRelation: {
    key: 'invoice'
  }
}]
});
```

4. To initialize models with a one-to-many relationship, pass the invoice items' data in a single JSON when creating a new `InvoiceModel` object instance.

```
var invoiceModel = new InvoiceModel
  ({
    referenceNumber: '12345',
    date: '2012-09-01',
    items: [
      { description:'Wooden Toy House', price:22, quantity:3 },
      { description:'Farm Animal Set', price:17, quantity:1 }
    ]
  });

invoiceModel.get('items').at(0).get('description');
// Wooden Toy House

invoiceModel.get('items').at(0).get('invoice')
.get('referenceNumber'); // 12345
```

5. Add new records into this relation with the help of the `add()` method when accessing the related collection using the `items` attribute.

```
// Add new model to a collection
invoiceModel.get('items').add
  ({
    description: 'Powerboat',
    price: 12,
    quantity: 1
  });

invoiceModel.get('items').at(2).get('invoice') == invoiceModel;
// true
```

Or we can also create an instance of `invoiceItemModel` and set the invoice attribute with an instance of `invoiceModel`; thus, a new relation in both the directions will be created.

```
// Add new model
invoiceItemModel = new InvoiceItemModel
  ({
    description: 'Jet Ski',
    price: 12,
    quantity: 1,
    invoice: invoiceModel
  });

invoiceModel.get('items').at(3).get('description');
// Jet Ski
```

How it works...

Each `Backbone.RelationalModel` registers itself with `Backbone.Store` upon creation, and is removed from `Store` when destroyed. When creating or updating an attribute that is a key in a relation, the removed related objects are notified of their removal, and new related objects are looked up in `Store`.

There's more...

In this section, we are going to learn some advanced usages of `Backbone.Relational`.

Implementing a many-to-many relationship

There is no way to create a many-to-many relationship between two models out of the box, but it can be easily done with the help of a pair of one-to-many relationships between those models and a new intermediate model.

Exporting related models to JSON

When exporting a model to JSON, it does include related models. This is how we can export `InvoiceModel` to JSON.

```
JSON.stringify(invoiceModel.toJSON());
```

And here is a result of such an export.

```
{
  "referenceNumber":"12345",
  "date":"2012-09-01",
```

```
   "items":[
      {
         "description":"Wooden Toy House","price":22,"quantity":3
      },
      {"description":"Farm Animal Set","price":17,"quantity":1},
      {"description":"Powerboat","price":12,"quantity":1},
      {"description":"Jet Ski","price":12,"quantity":1}
   ]
}
```

This is how we can export the `InvoiceItemModel` model.

```
JSON.stringify(invoiceModel.get('items').at(0).toJSON())
```

And the result is the following code snippet:

```
{
   "description":"Wooden Toy House",
   "price":22,
   "quantity":3,
   "invoice":{includeInJSON
      "referenceNumber":"12345",
      "date":"2012-09-01",
      "items":[
         null,
         {
            "description":"Farm Animal Set","price":17,
            "quantity":1
         },
         {"description":"Powerboat","price":12,"quantity":1},
         {"description":"Jet Ski","price":12,"quantity":1}
      ]
   }
}
```

As we can see, the `toJSON()` method also exports reversed relationships, but we can control the attributes of the related models that need to be exported by specifying an array of such attributes in the `includeInJSON` property for direct and reverse relationships.

```
var InvoiceModel = Backbone.RelationalModel.extend
   ({
      relations: [{
         type: Backbone.HasMany,
         key: 'items',
```

```
    relatedModel: InvoiceItemModel,
    collectionType: InvoiceItemCollection,

    // Restrict related models properties when exporting
    // to JSON.
    includeInJSON: ['description', 'price', 'quantity'],

    reverseRelation: {
      key: 'invoice',

      // Restrict related models properties when exporting
      // to JSON for reversed relations.
      includeInJSON: ['referenceNumber', 'items'],
    }
  }]
});
```

See also

- ▶ *Implementing a one-to-one relationship* in *Chapter 2, Models*

- ▶ More information about exporting to JSON is described in the *Synchronizing models and collections with a RESTful service* recipe in *Chapter 7, REST and Storage*

- ▶ A complete documentation of the Backbone-relational extension can be found on its GitHub page at `https://github.com/PaulUithol/Backbone-relational`

- ▶ Also, there is an alternative to the Backbone-relational extension, which is Backbone-associations

4
Views

In this chapter, we will cover the following areas:

- ▶ Rendering a view
- ▶ Dealing with a view element using jQuery
- ▶ Rendering a model in a view
- ▶ Rendering a collection in a view
- ▶ Splitting a view into subviews
- ▶ Handling **Document Object Model** (**DOM**) events in a view
- ▶ Switching views using Backbone.Router

Introduction

This chapter is devoted to the view object in Backbone.js; it is used for rendering data into HTML code. A view can be bound to the HTML element in the DOM tree and can handle its events and events for its child elements.

Models and collections are typically rendered with the help of a view that acts as an interactive bridge between business logic and a user. For example, a view can listen to DOM events and as a result, manipulate models and collections or navigate the user to a different page. The process can also go in a reverse direction: changes in models and collections trigger a view update, and so changes in a DOM tree are made.

A Backbone view relies on frontend JavaScript libraries, such as jQuery or Zepto when dealing with HTML elements and handling their events.

Rendering a view

When we want to output any data to the user, we should typically do it with the help of a Backbone view. In this recipe, we are going to create a simple view and render it.

Our result will look like the following screenshot:

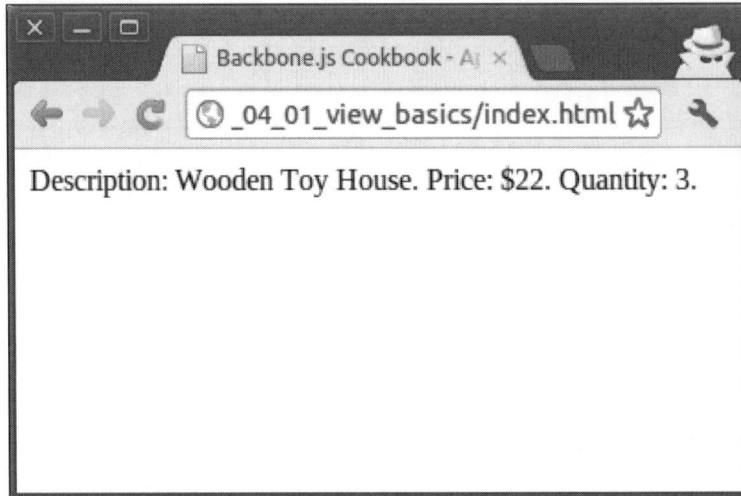

How to do it...

Follow the ensuing steps to create a simple view and render it.

1. Define a new view by extending the `Backbone.View` object:

```
var InvoiceItemView = Backbone.View.extend({

  // HTML element name, where to render a view.
  el: 'body',

  // Initialize view object values.
  initialize: function() {
    this.html = 'Description: Wooden Toy House. ' +
      'Price: $22. Quantity: 3.'
  },

  // Render view.
  render: function() {
```

```
        // Set html for the view element using jQuery.
        $(this.el).html(this.html);
    }
});
```

2. Create an instance of the view:

```
var invoiceItemView = new InvoiceItemView();
```

3. Call the `render()` method manually to output HTML code to the user:

```
invoiceItemView.render();
```

How it works...

In the `initialize()` method of the view, we generate the HTML code and save it in the `html` property, which we have been using lately in the `render()` method, where we assign this code to the HTML container defined by the `el` property. To do so, we invoke jQuery functions, such as `$()` and `html()`.

When a new view instance is created, the `initialize()` method is triggered automatically. Additionally, we can pass any standard property to the view from outside of the object when creating its instance. It can be done with the help of the following code snippet:

```
var invoiceItemView = new InvoiceItemView({
    el: 'body'
});
```

The `el` property can also be defined as a function if we want it to be calculated dynamically.

When the `render()` method is called, it runs our code that then renders the view.

There's more...

In this section, we will learn some useful tricks when dealing with a view.

Creating a new HTML element associated with a view

Sometimes, we may not want to render a view into the existing HTML element in the DOM tree; instead, we may want to create a new one and then add it to the document. Follow the given steps to create a new HTML element associated with a view.

1. Define a view and set its elements and attributes manually by assigning values to the `tagName`, `className`, and `attributes` properties:

```
// Define new view.
var InvoiceItemView2 = Backbone.View.extend({
```

```
        // Set tag name and its attributes.
        tagName: 'p',
        className: 'item',
        attributes: {
          'align': 'left'
        },

        // Initialize view object values.
        initialize: function() {
          this.html = 'Farm Animal Set. Price: $17. Quantity: 1.'
        },

        // Render view.
        render: function() {

          // Set html for the view element using jQuery.
          $(this.el).html(this.html);
        }
      });
```

2. Create a new view instance. When doing this, Backbone will automatically assign `el` with an appropriate value:

    ```
    // Create new view instance.
    var invoiceItemView2 = new InvoiceItemView2();

    invoiceItemView2.el; // <p align="left" class="item"></p>
    ```

3. Render this view. Our render code will create a new HTML object:

    ```
    invoiceItemView2.render();
    ```

4. Insert the newly created HTML object into the DOM:

    ```
    $('body').append(invoiceItemView2.el);
    ```

5. Check the result. The body of our HTML page should contain a code like the following code snippet:

```
<body>
    <p align="left" class="item">
        Farm Animal Set. Price: $17. Quantity: 1.
    </p>
</body>
```

Changing the view element dynamically

We may want to change the view element during the working of our code. This could be done with the help of a `setElement()` method. Both of the following are valid.

```
// Change existing element to the new one.
InvoiceItemView.setElement('li');

// Change existing element to the one already exists
// in the DOM tree.
InvoiceItemView.setElement($('body div'));
```

When calling the `setElement()` method, Backbone undelegates events assigned to a previous element, and assigns them to a new element.

Removing a view

When we have finished working with a view and want to remove it, we also need to remove its elements from the DOM and stop listening to events. To do this, we simply need to call the `remove()` method.

See also

> ▶ In this recipe, we use the jQuery method `$()` to access the properties of the view element. Please refer to the next recipe to get more information about jQuery.

Dealing with a view element using jQuery

There is no doubt that jQuery is the most popular JavaScript library nowadays. It simplifies document traversing with the help of CSS selectors, and provides easy event handling, animating, and AJAX interactions.

Backbone.js relies on jQuery when dealing with a view. In this recipe, we are going to learn how to interact with a view element using jQuery.

How to do it...

Follow the given steps to deal with a view element using jQuery.

1. To access a view element with jQuery, use `$(this.el)`:

   ```
   $(this.el).show();
   ```

2. Use `this.$el` as a shortened alias for `$(this.el)`:

   ```
   this.$el.appendl('<li>An item</li>');
   ```

3. To run a query within the scope of a view, use `this.$el.find()`:

   ```
   this.$el.find('li').html('Hey there');
   ```

4. Use `this.$()` as a shortened alias for `this.$el.find()`:

   ```
   this.$el('li').addClass('highlighted');
   ```

How it works...

Backbone integrates with the jQuery library as well as with Zepto.js and Ender.js. When Backbone is loaded, it determines which library is used and assigns a reference to it in the form of the `Backbone.$` variable.

There are a couple of aliases, such as `this.$el` and `this.$()`, that simplify access to the library.

There's more...

In this section, we are going to meet a jQuery alternative known as Zepto.

Using Zepto as a faster alternative to jQuery

Zepto is a minimalist JavaScript library that is 99 percent compatible with jQuery. The design goal of Zepto was to have a small-sized library and faster execution rate, which can be achieved by supporting modern browsers only. As a result, Zepto works much faster on mobile devices.

To use Zepto with Backbone, you need to perform the following steps:

1. Download the library from `http://zeptojs.com` and include it in the `lib` folder of your project.

2. Include Zepto in the `index.html` file instead of in jQuery.

   ```
   <script src="lib/zepto.js"></script>
   ```

See also

► You can find the complete documentation of jQuery on its official website `http://jquery.com`.

Rendering a model in a view

When working with models, we may often want to render them and show them in the browser. Typically, this can be done by creating a view for rendering a model and passing the model instance as a parameter.

In this recipe, we are going to render a simple model with a view, and the result will look like the following screenshot:

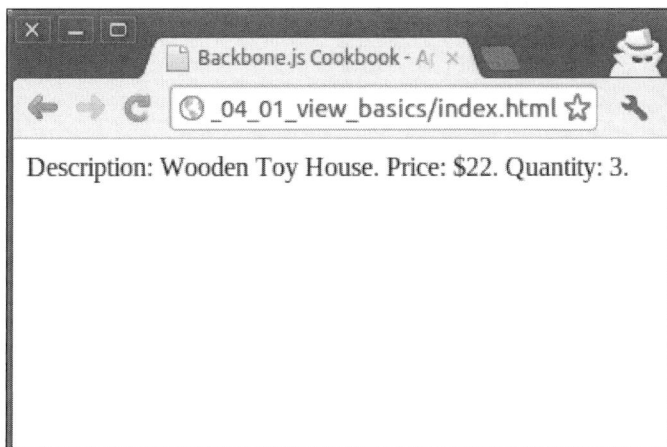

How to do it...

Follow the given steps to render a model in a view.

1. Define a new model:

```
var InvoiceItemModel = Backbone.Model.extend({

});
```

2. Define a view that will render this model:

```
var InvoiceItemView = Backbone.View.extend({

  // HTML element name, where to render a view.
  el: 'body',

  // Render view.
  render: function() {
    var html = 'Description: ' +
```

```
        this.model.get('description') + '. ' +
        'Price: ' + this.model.get('price') + '. ' +
        'Quantity: ' + this.model.get('quantity') + '.';


        // Set html for the view element using jQuery.
        $(this.el).html(html);
      }
    });
```

3. Create a model instance:

```
    var invoiceItemModel = new InvoiceItemModel({
        description: 'Farmer Figure',
        price: 8,
        quantity: 1
    });
```

4. Create a view instance and pass the model to it as a parameter:

```
    var invoiceItemView = new InvoiceItemView({

        // Pass model as a parameter to a view.
        model: invoiceItemModel
    });
```

5. Render the view:

```
    invoiceItemView.render();
```

How it works...

When initializing a new view object, we pass a model object to the view that is added to its property array by Backbone. In any method of this view, the assigned model can be made available by using the `this.model` property.

See also

▶   Often when rendering a model in a view, we need to update HTML if the model object has to get updated. This means we need to call the `setElement()` method every time the model is changed. Fortunately, Backbone provides an event-handling mechanism that does this automatically. It has been described in *Chapter 5, Events and Bindings*.

Rendering a collection in a view

In this recipe, we are going to learn a simple way of rendering a collection of models in the view.

The result output is an HTML list and looks like the following screenshot:

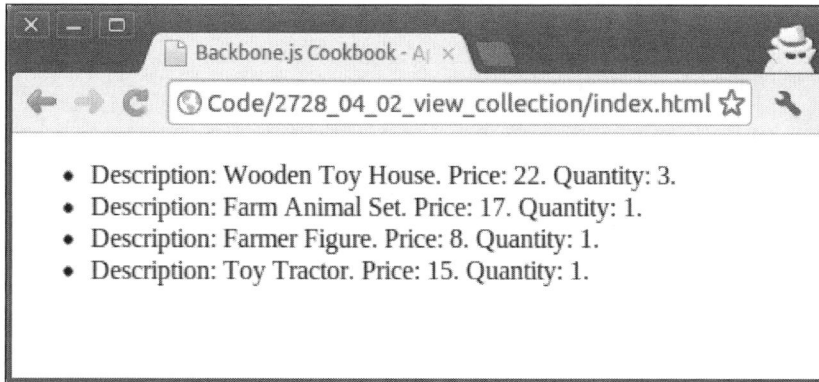

How to do it...

Follow the given steps to render a collection in a view.

1. Define a model:

```
var InvoiceItemModel = Backbone.Model.extend({

});
```

2. Define a collection:

```
var InvoiceItemCollection = Backbone.Collection.extend({
  model: InvoiceItemModel
});
```

3. Define a view:

```
var InvoiceItemListView = Backbone.View.extend({

  // HTML element name, where to render a view.
  el: 'body',

  // Render view.
  render: function() {
    var html = '';
```

```
    _.each(this.collection.models,function(model,index,list) {
      var item_html = 'Description: ' +
        model.get('description') + '. ' +
        'Price: ' + model.get('price') + '. ' +
        'Quantity: ' + model.get('quantity') + '.';
      html = html + '<li>' + item_html + '</li>';
    });

    html = '<ul>' + html + '</ul>';

    // Set html for the view element using jQuery.
    $(this.el).html(html);
    }
  });
```

4. Create a collection instance:

```
var invoiceItemCollection = new InvoiceItemCollection([
  { description: 'Wooden Toy House', price: 22, quantity: 3 },
  { description: 'Farm Animal Set', price: 17, quantity: 1 },
  { description: 'Farmer Figure', price: 8, quantity: 1 },
  { description: 'Toy Tractor', price: 15, quantity: 1 }
]);
```

5. Create a view instance:

```
var invoiceItemListView = new InvoiceItemListView({

  // Pass model as a parameter to a view.
  collection: invoiceItemCollection
});
```

6. Render a view:

```
invoiceItemListView.render();
```

How it works...

When initializing a new view object, we pass the collection object to it, so that we later handle in a loop with the help of the `render()` method. Thus, we create the result HTML code that is later assigned to the view element.

See also

▶   Often when rendering a collection in a view, we need to update HTML if the collection is being sorted or updated. This means we need to call the `setElement()` method every time the model is changed. Fortunately, Backbone provides an event-handling mechanism that does this automatically. It has been described in *Chapter 5, Events and Bindings*.

Splitting a view into subviews

In the previous recipe, we used a single big view to render the collection. However, there is a better way to handle big views, by splitting them into multiple small views. Such a practice should have several advantages. In the context of our collection, the following advantages are observed:

- The ability to insert, delete, or update a model in a collection without the need to re-render the whole collection
- The ability to re-use subviews in other places of the program
- The ability to split a single big piece of code into small and simple parts

Quantity	Description	Price	Total
3	Wooden Toy House	22	66
1	Farm Animal Set	17	17
1	Farmer Figure	8	8
1	Toy Tractor	15	15

In this recipe, we are going to split a view which renders a collection into several simple subviews. Let's output the data in a table rather than in a list and apply some **Cascading Style Sheets** (**CSS**) to make it look better.

How to do it...

Follow the given steps to split one big view into small subviews.

1. Make sure you have the model and the collection definition:

```
var InvoiceItemModel = Backbone.Model.extend({

});
```

```
      var InvoiceItemCollection = Backbone.Collection.extend({
        model: InvoiceItemModel
      });
```

2.   Define a view for rendering a single model:

```
      // Define new view to render a model.
      var InvoiceItemView = Backbone.View.extend({

        // Define element tag name.
        tagName: 'tr',

        // Render view.
        render: function() {

          // Add cells to the table row.
          $(this.el).html(_.map([
            this.model.get('quantity'),
            this.model.get('description'),
            this.model.get('price'), this.model.calculateAmount(),
          ], function(val, key){
            return '<td>' + val + '</td>'
          }));

          return this;
        }
      });
```

3.   Define a view for rendering a collection:

```
      // Define new view to render a collection.
      var InvoiceItemListView = Backbone.View.extend({

        // Define element tag name.
        tagName: 'table',

        // Define element class name.
        className: 'invoice-item-view',

        // Render view.
        render: function() {

          $(this.el).empty();

          // Append table with a table header.
          $(this.el).append($('<tr></tr>').html(
```

```
        _.map(['Quantity', 'Description', 'Price', 'Total'],
          function(val, key){
            return '<th>' + val + '</th>'
        })
      ));

      // Append table  with a row.
      $(this.el).append(
        _.map(this.collection.models, function(model, key) {
          return new InvoiceItemView({
            model: model
          }).render().el;
        })
      );

      return this;
    }
  });
```

4. Define a view for rendering a whole page.

```
    var InvoiceItemListPageView = Backbone.View.extend({

      // Render whole page view.
      render: function() {
        $(this.el).html(new InvoiceItemListView({
          collection: this.collection
        }).render().el);
      }
    });
```

5. Create and initialize a collection instance with data.

```
    var invoiceItemCollection = new InvoiceItemCollection([
      { description: 'Wooden Toy House', price: 22, quantity: 3 },
      { description: 'Farm Animal Set', price: 17, quantity: 1 },
      { description: 'Farmer Figure', price: 8, quantity: 1 },
      { description: 'Toy Tractor', price: 15, quantity: 1 }
    ]);
```

6. Create a view instance for a whole page and render it.

```
    new InvoiceItemListPageView({
      collection: invoiceItemCollection,
      el: 'body'
    }).render();
```

How it works...

In this example, we used `InvoiceItemView` for rendering the model and `InvoiceItemListView` for rendering the collection.

Also, we introduced the new view `InvoiceItemListPageView` that renders the whole page. When creating an instance of this view, we pass the `el` property; it contains the HTML element name where the view should output its result. This gives us more flexibility, and so we can render the view wherever we need.

Handling Document Object Model (DOM) events in a view

A view in Backbone provides some functionality to interact with a user. It allows the handling of events that occur in the DOM in context of the view element.

In this recipe, we are going to modify an example given in the previous recipe. Let's add an **Edit** button to each row of the table as shown in the following screenshot:

Quantity	Description	Price	Total	Operations
3	Wooden Toy House	22	66	Edit
1	Farm Animal Set	17	17	Edit
1	Farmer Figure	8	8	Edit
1	Toy Tractor	15	15	Edit

By clicking on the **Edit** button, we will immediately replace the text values with input boxes so that the user can enter new values. We will also show **Save** and **Cancel** buttons to save or cancel the changes.

If the user clicks on the **Save** button, the model gets updated. If the user clicks on the **Cancel** button, values in the row are restored. Clicking on both the buttons makes the row view work in the view mode again.

How to do it...

Apply the following changes to `InvoiceItemView` that we created in the previous recipe.

1. Define a view:

```
// Define new view to render a model.
var InvoiceItemView = Backbone.View.extend({

    // Define tag name.
    tagName: 'tr',
});
```

2. Introduce a rendering function when the user is viewing an item:

```
renderViewMode: function() {
  $(this.el).html(_.map([
    this.model.get('quantity'),
    this.model.get('description'),
    this.model.get('price'),
    this.model.calculateAmount(),
    '<button class="edit">Edit</button>'
```

```
    ], function(val, key){
      return '<td>' + val + '</td>'
    }));
  },
```

3. Introduce a rendering function when the user is editing an item:

```
renderEditMode: function() {
  $(this.el).html(_.map([
    '<input class="quantity" value="' +
      this.model.get('quantity') + '">',
    '<input class="description" value="' +
      this.model.get('description') +
      '">',
    '<input class="price" value="' +
      this.model.get('price') + '">',
    this.model.calculateAmount(),
    '<button class="save">Save</button>' +
    '<button class="cancel">Cancel</button>'
  ], function(val, key){
    return '<td>' + val + '</td>'
  }));
},
```

4. Set a property that will contain a function name that will be called on rendering the view:

```
renderCallback: 'renderViewMode',

render: function() {
  this[this.renderCallback]();

  return this;
},
```

5. Map the DOM events to the handlers:

```
events: {
  'click button.edit': 'edit',
  'click button.save': 'save',
  'click button.cancel': 'cancel',
},
```

6. Define the event handlers:

```
// Edit button click handler.
edit: function() {
```

```
        this.renderCallback = 'renderEditMode';

        this.render();
      },

      // Save button click handler.
      save: function() {
        this.model.set({
          quantity: $(this.el).find('input.quantity').val(),
          description:
            $(this.el).find('input.description').val(),
          price: $(this.el).find('input.price').val(),
        });

        this.renderCallback = 'renderViewMode';

        this.render();
      },

      // Cancel button click handler.
      cancel: function() {
        this.renderCallback = 'renderViewMode';

        this.render();
      }
```

7. Create and initialize a collection instance with data:

```
var invoiceItemCollection = new InvoiceItemCollection([
  { description: 'Wooden Toy House', price: 22, quantity: 3 },
  { description: 'Farm Animal Set', price: 17, quantity: 1 },
  { description: 'Farmer Figure', price: 8, quantity: 1 },
  { description: 'Toy Tractor', price: 15, quantity: 1 }
]);
```

8. Create a view instance for a whole page and render it:

```
    new InvoiceItemListPageView({
      collection: invoiceItemCollection,
      el: 'body'
    }).render();
```

How it works...

By defining the `event` property, we can tell Backbone how to map events to the handlers. To do so, we will use the following syntax:

```
{"event selector": "callback"}
```

Backbone.js uses jQuery's `on()` function to provide declarative callbacks for DOM events within a view. If the `selector` value is not given, the view's root element (`this.el`) is assumed.

There's more...

This section describes view methods to delegate and undelegate DOM events.

Delegating and undelegating events manually

In some cases, we may need a view to start handling DOM events manually from a specific place in the program. This can be done by calling the `delegateEvents()` method. It accepts a hash table of event names and their callbacks. If no parameter is given, `this.events` is used.

If we need a view to stop handling DOM events, we should call the `undelegateEvents()` method. This can be useful when we hide the view temporarily and need to ensure that no unexpected behavior is caused by the DOM events.

See also...

> ▸ A complete reference to the jQuery events can be found at `http://api.jquery.com/category/events/`.

Switching views using Backbone.Router

In the real Backbone application, we'll often need to switch from one view to another. This is typically done with the help of Backbone.Router; it allows us to map a URL to the specific callback that renders a view. In *Chapter 1, Understanding Backbone*, we learned about a router in Backbone.js. However, we did not speak much about its interaction with views.

In this recipe, we are going to build a Backbone application that will dynamically render an appropriate view on the URL, as well as change and remove the view that was shown to the user previously in order to prevent a memory leak. The views are going to be switched without a page reload, because Backbone.Router supports hash URLs and `pushState`.

In our application, we are going to implement `InvoiceListView` and `InvoicePageView`. The first one displays a list of invoices, as shown in the following screenshot:

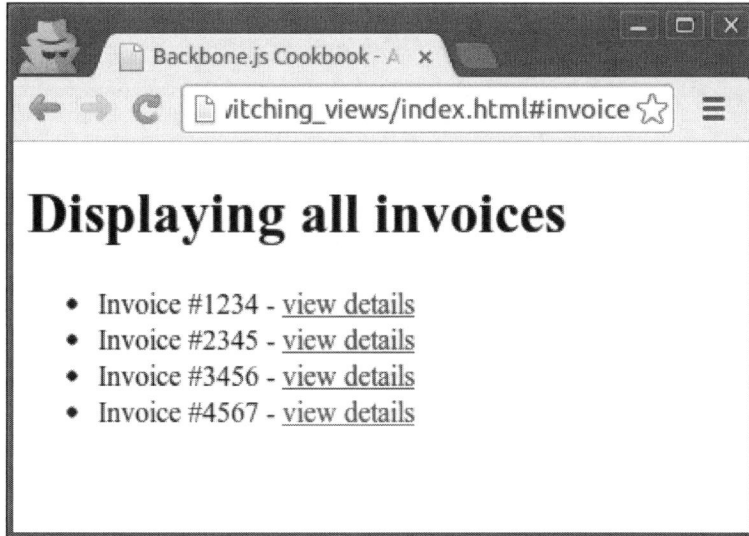

When the user clicks on the **view details** link, he/she is shown an invoice details screen like the one shown in the following screenshot:

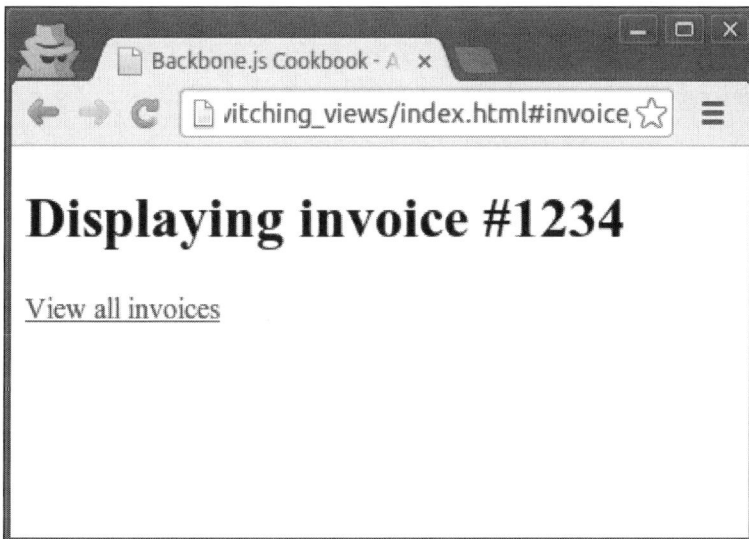

How to do it...

Let's assume that we already have a model, a collection, and view objects defined. Follow the given steps to create a router that switches views.

1. Define a router object and its routes:

```
var Workspace = Backbone.Router.extend({

    // Define routes
    routes: {
      '': 'invoiceList',
      'invoice': 'invoiceList',
      'invoice/:id': 'invoicePage',
    }
```

2. Create a new collection instance in the `initialize()` method in the router object:

```
initialize: function() {

    //  Create collection
    this.invoiceCollection = new InvoiceCollection([
      { referenceNumber: 1234},
      { referenceNumber: 2345},
      { referenceNumber: 3456},
      { referenceNumber: 4567}
    ]);
}
```

3. Define routing callbacks in the router object:

```
invoiceList: function() {
    this.changeView(new InvoiceListView({
      collection: this.invoiceCollection
    }));
},

invoicePage: function(id) {
    this.changeView(new InvoicePageView({
      model: this.invoiceCollection.get(id)
    }));
}
```

4. Define a `changeView()` method in the router object that will help us change the current view:

```
changeView: function(view) {
    if (this.currentView) {
        if (this.currentView == view) {
            return;
        }

        this.currentView.remove();
    }

    $('body').append(view.render().el);

    this.currentView = view;
    }
});
```

5. Create a router instance and run the `Backbone.history.start()` method to start our application:

```
new Workspace();
Backbone.history.start();
```

How it works...

Many interesting things are happening in the `changeView()` method. Just for our assurance, we check if the current view is not the one to which we are going to switch and then remove. While removing a view, all the events handled by it need to be unbound, and the corresponding HTML elements removed from the DOM tree. Then, we render a new view and append its element to the body.

Removing previously used views helps us to avoid memory leaks, which can happen when the application is used continuously for a very long time.

See also

▸ Please refer to *Chapter 1*, *Understanding Backbone*, to learn more about routers in Backbone.js.

5

Events and Bindings

In this chapter, we will cover:

- ▶ Managing events in `Backbone.js`
- ▶ Handling events of Backbone objects
- ▶ Binding a model to a view
- ▶ Binding a collection to a view
- ▶ Bidirectional binding with `Backbone.stickit`
- ▶ Binding a model and a collection to a select list
- ▶ Handling keyboard shortcuts in a view
- ▶ Handling router events

Introduction

This chapter is devoted to the `Backbone.Events` object and its involvement in other Backbone objects, such as models, collections, views, and routers.

We will learn how to assign a callback to a specific event or how to listen to events of other objects. We will also learn how to bind a model or a collection to a view in both directions. So if a model is updated, the view automatically shows the changes, or if a user inputs data into a view, the model is validated and updated.

Managing events in Backbone.js

Backbone provides a unified way for triggering and handling events in other Backbone objects, such as `Model`, `Collection`, `View`, and `Router`. This becomes possible due to the `Backbone.Events` object, which provides this functionality and thus can be mixed to any object, including your own.

In this recipe, we are going to learn how to mix `Backbone.Events` to your own object, how to trigger an event, and how to bind a callback to an event.

How to do it...

Perform the following steps to handle object events.

1. Define a new object.

   ```
   object1 = {};
   ```

2. Mix `Backbone.Events` to your object.

   ```
   _.extend(object1, Backbone.Events);
   ```

3. Define a callback function.

   ```
   var hello = function(msg) {
     alert("Hello"+ msg);
   }
   ```

4. Bind the callback using the `on()` method.

   ```
   object1.on("handshake", hello);
   ```

   Alternatively, you can use the `once()` method to fire the callback once before it is unbound.

   ```
   object1.once("handshake", hello);
   ```

   > If you have a large number of different events for an object, the convention is to use colons to name them `poll:start`, or `change:selection`.

5. Trigger an event by calling the `trigger()` method.

   ```
   object1.trigger("handshake", "world!");
   ```

How it works...

In the `on()` method, `Backbone.Events` saves callback in an associative array `_events`, and then in the `trigger()` method it runs all callbacks for that event iteratively.

There's more...

In this section, we will learn some important topics about events: unbinding callback from the event and listening events of other objects.

Unbinding callback from the event

To unbind callbacks from the event, we need to use the `off()` method. The following line of code will unbind a specific callback we set previously.

```
object1.off("handshake", hello);
```

To unbind all callbacks from the event, skip the second parameter.

```
object1.off("handshake");
```

To unbind a specific callback from all events, skip the first parameter.

```
object1.off(null, hello);
```

To unbind all callbacks from all events, skip both parameters.

```
object1.off();
```

Listening to events on other objects

To listen to events on other objects, we can use the `listenTo()` method.

```
object2.listenTo(object1, 'handshake', object2.hello);
```

It works similar to the `on()` method, but its advantage is that it allows us to keep a track of the events, and they can be removed all at once later on.

```
object2.stopListening(object1);
```

To stop listening to all objects, run the `stopListening()` method without parameters.

```
object2.stopListening();
```

Handling events of Backbone objects

All Backbone objects implement `Backbone.Events`, and some of them provide built-in events, to which your objects can listen.

For example, a `change` event is fired when a model is changed. Especially for this event, there are several methods in `Backbone.Model` that can be used in the `change` event callback. In this recipe, we are going to learn how to use them.

How to do it...

Perform the following steps to handle model events.

1. Create a new `model` instance.

    ```
    var model = new Backbone.Model({
       firstName: 'John',
       lastName: 'Doe',
       age: 20,
    });
    ```

2. Bind the callback to the `change` event.

    ```
    model.on('change', function(model) {

    }
    ```

3. Use the `hasChanged()` method in the event callback to check if the specific attribute has been changed since the last `change` event.

    ```
    model.hasChanged("age"); // true
    model.hasChanged("firstName"); // false
    ```

4. Use the `changedAttributes()` method in the event callback to obtain changed attributes' hash.

    ```
    model.changedAttributes(); // Object {age: 21}
    ```

5. Use the `previous()` method in the event callback to get the value of the previous attribute.

    ```
    model.previous('age'); // 20
    ```

6. Use the `previousAttributes()` method in the event callback to get the hash of the previous attributes.

    ```
    model.previousAttributes();
       // Object {firstName: "John", lastName: "Doe", age:
          20}
    ```

7. Change a `model` attribute to trigger the `change` event.

    ```
    model.set('age', 21);
    ```

There's more...

In this section, we are going to learn more about events to Backbone objects: avoiding event triggering when working with Backbone objects and using built-in events.

Avoiding event triggering when working with Backbone objects

There is a way to avoid event triggering when working with Backbone events. This can be helpful if you want to update object properties without making event callbacks know about this fact.

For example, you can pass {silent: true} when updating model values.

```
model.set('age', 22, {silent: true});
```

The following line of code is also valid:

```
model.set({ age: 25 }, {silent: true});
```

Using built-in events

The following events are used with model objects:

- **change** (model, options): It is fired when a model's attributes have changed
- **change:[attribute]** (model, value, options): It is fired when a specific attribute has been updated
- **destroy** (model, collection, options): It is fired when a model is destroyed
- **invalid** (model, error, options): It is fired when a model's validation fails on the client
- **error** (model, xhr, options): It is fired when a model's save call fails on the server
- **sync** (model, resp, options): It is fired when a model has been successfully synced with the server

The following events are used with collections:

- **add** (model, collection, options): It is fired when a model is added to a collection
- **remove** (model, collection, options): It is fired when a model is removed from a collection
- **reset** (collection, options): It is fired when the entire content of the collection has been replaced
- **sort** (collection, options): It is fired when the collection has been re-sorted
- **sync** (collection, resp, options): It is fired when a collection has been successfully synced with the server

The following events are used with the router object:

- **route:[name]** (params): It is fired by the router when a specific route is matched
- **route** (router, route, params): It is fired by history (or router) when any route has been matched

The following events are triggered when storage operations are performed:

- **route:[name]** (params): It is fired by the router when a specific route is matched
- **route** (router, route, params): It is fired by history (or router) when any route has been matched

To handle any triggered event, use the special event `all`.

See also

- You can find the complete built-in events catalog from `http://backbonejs.org/#Events-catalog`
- To check which Backbone methods support `{silent: true}`, please refer to the official docs

Binding a model to a view

One of the useful features in `Backbone.js` is the ability to bind model changes to a view, thus a view is re-rendered every time a model is changed. It allows you to write less code and makes your application work like an AJAX app, for example, when new data is fetched from a REST server, the user sees the update immediately.

Let's take an example of the *Rendering a model in a view* recipe from *Chapter 4, Views*, where we rendered a model with a view and modified it, so views is re-rendered every time the model is updated.

The view which we are going to implement will be rendered as shown in the following screenshot:

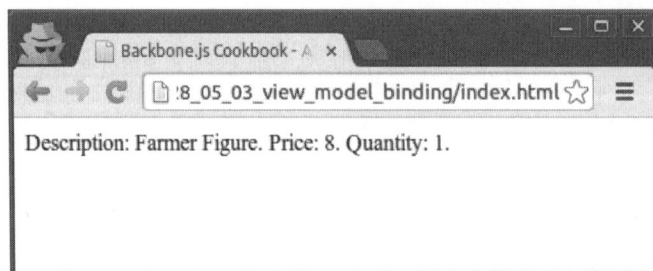

In the browser console, we can modify the model values, thus the `change` event is triggered and the view is re-rendered.

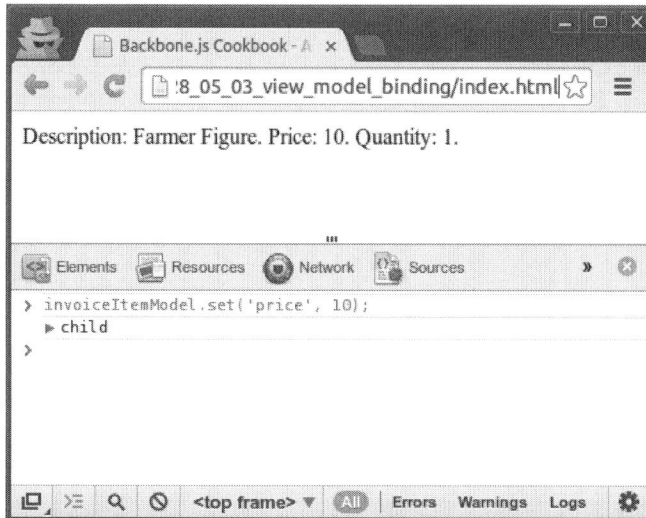

Description: Farmer Figure. Price: 10. Quantity: 1.

How to do it...

Perform the following steps to bind a model to a view.

1. Define a new model.

```
var InvoiceItemModel = Backbone.Model.extend({

});
```

2. Define a view that renders this model.

```
var InvoiceItemView = Backbone.View.extend({

  // HTML element name, where to render a view.
  el: 'body',

  // Render view.
  render: function() {
    var html = 'Description: ' +
      this.model.get('description') + '. ' +
      'Price: ' + this.model.get('price') + '. ' +
      'Quantity: ' + this.model.get('quantity') + '.';
```

```
                    // Set html for the view element using jQuery.
                    $(this.el).html(html);
                }
            });
```

3. Bind the model to `InvoiceItemView` in the `initialize()` method.

    ```
    initialize: function() {
        this.listenTo(this.model, 'change', this.render, this);
    }
    ```

4. Create the model instance.

    ```
    var invoiceItemModel = new InvoiceItemModel({
        description: 'Farmer Figure',
        price: 8,
        quantity: 1
    });
    ```

5. Create a view instance and pass `model` to it as a parameter.

    ```
    var invoiceItemView = new InvoiceItemView({

        // Pass model as a parameter to a view.
        model: invoiceItemModel
    });
    ```

6. Render the view.

    ```
    invoiceItemView.render();
    ```

7. To check how binding works, export the model to be a global variable, so we can update model values in a browser console.

    ```
    window.invoiceItemModel = invoiceItemModel;
    ```

How it works...

Both the `Backbone.Model` and `Backbone.View` objects implement `Backbone.Events`, so it is possible to listen to model changes in the view and bind the `render()` method as a callback for the `change` event.

Binding a collection to a view

In this recipe, we are going to learn how to bind a collection to a view. This can be very helpful if we have different views working with the same collection, or if we want to synchronize data with a REST server.

Let's take an example of the *Rendering a model in a view* recipe from *Chapter 4, Views*, where we rendered a collection with subviews and modified it. We are going to add an additional view with the **Add** and **Remove** buttons, which will update the collection.

Also, we will bind appropriate callbacks to the model and collection events in our first view, so it is re-rendered automatically when the collection is changed.

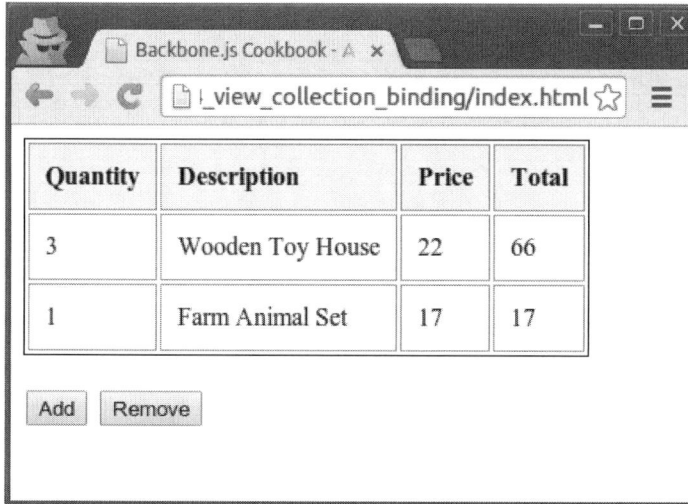

When a user clicks on the **Add** button, he/she is prompted to enter the required information to create `InvoiceItemModel`.

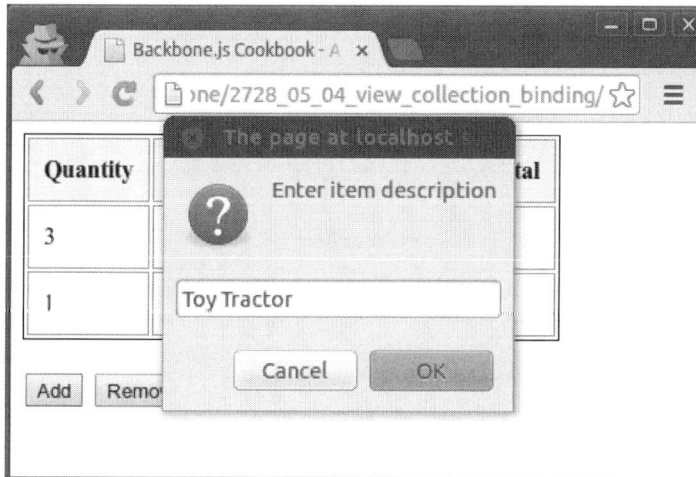

After the user goes through all the questions, a new model is created and added into a collection, and the corresponding views are updated.

When the **Remove** button is clicked, the user is promoted to enter the position of the item to be removed.

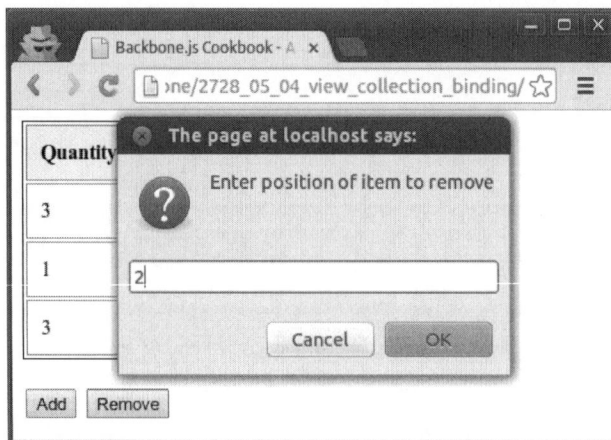

How to do it...

Perform the following steps to bind a collection to a view.

1. Make sure you have the model and collection definitions.

```
var InvoiceItemModel = Backbone.Model.extend({

});
```

```
var InvoiceItemCollection = Backbone.Collection.extend({
  model: InvoiceItemModel
});
```

2. Define a view for rendering a single model.

```
// Define new view to render a model.
var InvoiceItemView = Backbone.View.extend({

  // Define element tag name.
  tagName: 'tr',

  // Render view.
  render: function() {

    // Add cells to the table row.
    $(this.el).html(_.map([
      this.model.get('quantity'),
      this.model.get('description'),
      this.model.get('price'), this.model.calculateAmount(),
    ], function(val, key){
      return '<td>' + val + '</td>'
    }));

    return this;
  }
});
```

3. In the `initialize()` method of the `InvoiceItemView` object, bind callback to handle the `destroy` event of the model.

```
initialize: function() {
  this.listenTo(this.model, 'destroy', this.destroy, this);
}
```

4. Add the `destroy()` method, which removes the view bound to a model.

```
destroy: function() {
  this.remove();
}
```

5. Define a view for rendering a collection.

```
// Define new view to render a collection.
var InvoiceItemListView = Backbone.View.extend({

  // Define element tag name.
  tagName: 'table',
```

```
      // Define element class name.
      className: 'invoice-item-view',

      // Render view.
      render: function() {

        $(this.el).empty();

        // Append table with a table header.
        $(this.el).append($('<tr></tr>').html(
          _.map(['Quantity', 'Description', 'Price', 'Total'],
            function(val, key){
              return '<th>' + val + '</th>'
            }
          )
        ));

        // Append table  with a row.
        _.each(this.collection.models, function(model, key) {
          this.append(model);
        }, this);

        return this;
      },

      // Add invoice item row to the table.
      append: function(model) {
        $(this.el).append(
          new InvoiceItemView({ model: model }).render().el
        );
      }
    });
```

Here we used the `append()` method, which adds `InvoiceItemView` into the output table. We will use this method later on.

6. In the `initialize()` method of the `InvoiceItemListView` object, bind the callback to handle the `add` event of the collection.

```
    initialize: function() {
      this.listenTo(
        this.collection, 'add', this.append, this
      );
    },
```

Here we have called the same `append()` method.

7. Define the view with Add and Remove controls.

```javascript
var InvoiceItemListControlsView = Backbone.View.extend({
  render: function() {
    var html =
      '<br><input id="add" type="button"' value="Add" id>' +
      ' <input id="remove" type="button" value="Remove">';

    $(this.el).html(html);

    return this;
  },

  // Handle HTML events.
  events: {
    'click #add': 'addNewInvoiceItem',
    'click #remove': 'removeInvoiceItem',
  },

  // Add button handler.
  addNewInvoiceItem: function() {
    var description = prompt('Enter item description', '');
    var price = prompt('Enter item price', '0');
    var quantity = prompt('Enter item quantity', '1');

    this.collection.add([{
      description: description,
      price: price,
      quantity: quantity
    }]);
  },

  // Remove button handler.
  removeInvoiceItem: function() {
    var position =
      prompt('Enter position of item to remove', '');

    model = this.collection.at(position);
    model.destroy();
  }
});
```

8. Define a view for rendering a whole page.

```javascript
var InvoiceItemListPageView = Backbone.View.extend({

  // Render whole page view.
  render: function() {
```

```
        $(this.el).html(new InvoiceItemListView({
          collection: this.collection
        }).render().el);

        $(this.el).append(new InvoiceItemListControlsView({
          collection: this.collection
        }).render().el);
      }
    });
```

9. Create and initialize the collection instance with data.

```
    var invoiceItemCollection = new InvoiceItemCollection([
      { description: 'Wooden Toy House', price: 22, quantity: 3 },
      { description: 'Farm Animal Set', price: 17, quantity: 1 }
    ]);
```

10. Create the whole page view instance and render it.

```
        new InvoiceItemListPageView({
          collection: invoiceItemCollection,
          el: 'body'
        }).render();
```

How it works...

When a new model is added to the collection, the add event is fired, and the model is rendered as a table row and appended to the table.

When a model is destroyed, the destroy event is fired, and a view corresponding to this model is removed, also a view element is removed from a DOM tree.

Bidirectional binding with Backbone.stickit

In Backbone.js, we can bind a model to a view out of the box, but it is not easy to make binding in reverse direction without the need to parse values of HTML elements.

In this recipe, we will speak about the Backbone.stickit extension, which allows developers to implement bidirectional binding of the model properties and view elements in a simple and native Backbone.js way.

Among many similar extensions, Backbone.stickit stands out by its perfect documentation, simplicity, and the great advantage that it gives to application developers. It was written in New York Times not so long time ago, and its popularity is being growing day-by-day. It is definitely one of the coolest extensions for Backbone.js.

In this recipe, we are going to build a simple application that has a couple of views bound to the same model, so if a user makes changes in the element of the first view, the second view is updated automatically. The user interface of our application will look like the following screenshot:

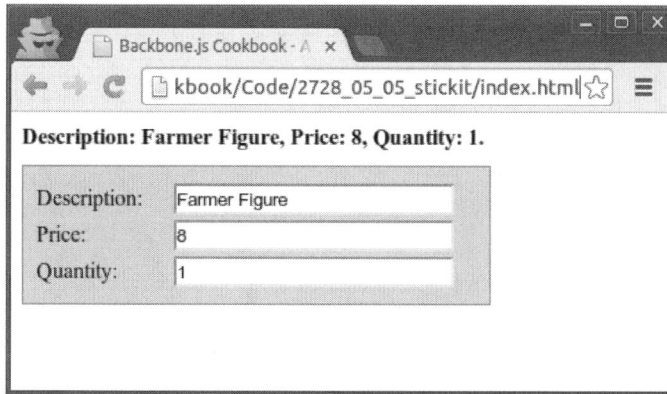

There are a couple of views that are bound to the same model. When the user enters data into the form, the model and the other view are updated.

Getting ready

You can download the `Backbone.stickit` extension from the **GitHub** page `https://github.com/nytimes/backbone.stickit`. To include this extension into your project, save the `backbone.stickit.js` file into the `lib` folder of your project and include the reference to this file in `index.html`.

> Including a Backbone extension into your project is described in detail in the *Extending an application with plugins* recipe in *Chapter 1, Understanding Backbone*.

How to do it...

Perform the following steps to perform a bidirectional binding.

1. Make sure you have a model defined.

```
var InvoiceItemModel = Backbone.Model.extend({

});
```

2. Define the form view.

```
var InvoiceItemFormView = Backbone.View.extend({

  // Define class name of view element.
  className: 'invoice-item-form-view',
});
```

3. Add the bindings hash to the view.

```
bindings: {
  '#description': 'description',
  '#price': 'price',
  '#quantity': 'quantity'
}
```

Here we used short binding definition, which acts as an alias for the detailed definition shown in the next snippet.

```
bindings: {
  '#description': { observe: 'description' },
  '#price': { observe: 'price' },
  '#quantity': { observe: 'quantity' }
}
```

4. Add the `render()` method to the view and call `this.stickit()` after rendering.

```
render: function() {
  var html = '<label>Description:</label>' +
    '<input type="text" id="description"></input><br>' +
    '<label>Price:</label>' +
    '<input type="text" id="price"></input><br>' +
    '<label>Quantity:</label>' +
    '<input type="text" id="quantity"></input><br>';

  // Set html for the view element using jQuery.
  $(this.el).html(html);

  // Here binding occurs.
  this.stickit();

  return this;
}
```

5. Define the other view in a similar way.

```
var InvoiceItemView = Backbone.View.extend({

  // Define class name of view element.
  className: 'invoice-item-view',
```

```
    // Bind HTML elements to the view model.
    bindings: {
      '#description': 'description',
      '#price': 'price',
      '#quantity': 'quantity'
    },

    // Render view.
    render: function() {
      var html = 'Description:' +
        '<span id="description"></span>, ' +
        'Price:  <span id="price"></span>, ' +
        'Quantity:  <span id="quantity"></span>.';

      // Set html for the view element using jQuery.
      $(this.el).html(html);

      // Here binding occurs.
      this.stickit();

      return this;
    },
  });
```

6. Create a new `model` instance.

```
    var invoiceItemModel = new InvoiceItemModel({
      description: 'Farmer Figure',
      price: 8,
      quantity: 1
    });
```

7. Append both views to the HTML body.

```
    $('body').append(new InvoiceItemView({
      model: invoiceItemModel
    }).render().el);
    $('body').append(new InvoiceItemFormView({
      model: invoiceItemModel
    }).render().el);
```

How it works...

Whenever the `stickit()` method is called, the stickit extension initializes `innerHTML` of the HTML elements, which we have defined in the bindings hash. Because of such initialization, Stickit lets us to keep our templates clean, and we don't need to pass model values into the `html` variable manually when rendering the view.

For the `InvoiceItemView` view, one-way binding is configured (model to view), so every time model properties get changed, the corresponding HTML elements are updated.

For the `InvoiceItemFormView` view, Stickit sets up two-way binding (model to view and then, view to model), connecting and reflecting changes in the view elements with changes in bound model attributes.

There's more...

This section describes advanced usage of the `Backbone.stickit` extension: overriding model getters and setters, overriding view element updates, and listening to a specific HTML event.

Overriding model getters and setters

When getting or setting properties of a model bound to our view, we can override the getting or setting behavior by specifying the `onGet` and `onSet` callbacks.

```
bindings: {
  '#price': {
    observe: 'price',
    onGet: 'priceGetter',
    onGet: 'priceSetter'
  }
},
priceGetter: function(val, options) {
  return '$ ' + val;
},
priceSetter: function(val, options) {
  return Number(val.replace(/[^0-9\.]+/g, ''));
}
```

Overriding view element updates

There are different ways in which we can override and customize view element updates. We can specify an `update` callback, which is triggered when an HTML element gets updated or we can specify `afterUpdate` callback, which will be executed afterwards.

```
bindings: {
  '#price': {
    observe: 'price',
    update: function($el, val, model, options) {
      $el.val(val);
    }
    afterUpdate: 'highlight',
  },
```

```
    },
    highlight: function($el, val, options) {
      $el.animate({ backgroundColor: "#ff9999" }, "fast")
        .animate({ backgroundColor: "#ffffff" }, "fast");
    }
  }
}
```

There is another way in which we can override value update for the view element by specifying updateMethod. By default it uses the text method, but we can change its value to html. If the html method is used, and we want to escape model values before assigning it to an HTML element, we can set the escape option to true.

```
bindings: {
  '#price': {
    observe: 'price',
    updateMethod: 'html',
    escape: true
  }
}
```

Listening to a specific HTML event

By default, for a textbox, textarea and other content-editable HTML elements, the Backbone. stickit extension listens to the following events, keyup, change, cut, and paste. For other elements, the Backbone.stickit extension listens to the change event.

However, there is a way to override this setting by specifying the events array.

```
bindings: {
  '#price': {
    observe: 'price',
    events: ['blur'],
  },
}
```

In this case, view-to-model binding will occur on the blur event of the #price textbox.

See also

- ► In the following recipe, we are going to continue learning about the Stickit extension. You can also find complete docs on Backbone.stickit on the **GitHub** page http://nytimes.github.com/backbone.stickit/.

Binding a model and a collection to a select list

In the previous recipe, we talked about how to bind a model to an HTML arbitrary element of the view. In this recipe we are going to learn how to bind a model to a select element. By changing the value of the select list, we need to change the associated property of a bound model.

This is a bit more complex, because we may want to take key-value pairs for select options from an array or a collection. Fortunately, the `Backbone.stickit` extension allows us to do this easily.

In this recipe, we will create a simple example to demonstrate how we can bind a model and a collection to a select list.

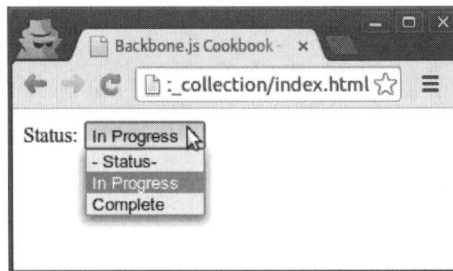

Getting ready

You can download the `Backbone.stickit` extension from the **GitHub** page `https://github.com/nytimes/backbone.stickit`. To include this extension into your project, save the `backbone.stickit.js` file into the `lib` folder and include the reference to it in `index.html`.

> Including the Backbone extension into your project is described in detail in the *Extending an application with plugins* recipe in *Chapter 1, Understanding Backbone*.

How to do it...

Perform the following steps to bind a model and a collection to a select list.

1. Define a model.

   ```
   var InvoiceModel = Backbone.Model.extend({
   });
   ```

2. Define a view.

```
var InvoiceView = Backbone.View.extend({

    // Define class name of view element.
    className: 'invoice-item-view',

    },

    // Render view.
    render: function() {
        var html = 'Status: <select id="items"></select>';

        // Set html for the view element using jQuery.
        $(this.el).html(html);

        // Here binding occurs.
        this.stickit();

        return this;
    },
});
```

3. Add bindings hash to the view.

```
    // Bind HTML elements to the view model.
    bindings: {
        'select#items': {
            observe: 'status',

            // Define additional options for select element.
            selectOptions: {

                // You can return regular Backbone collection or
                // an array of objects.
                collection: function() {
                    return [
                        {name: null, label: '- Status-'},
                        {name: 'in_progress', label: 'In Progress'},
                        {name: 'complete', label: 'Complete'}
                    ]
                },

                // Set the path to the label value for select
                // options within the collection of objects.
                labelPath: 'label',
```

```
            // Define the path to the values for select options
            // within the collection of objects.
            valuePath: 'name'
        }
    }
```

4. Create a new model instance.

```
    var invoiceModel = new InvoiceModel({
      status: 'in_progress'
    });
```

5. Render the view.

```
    $('body').append(new InvoiceView({
      model: invoiceModel
    }).render().el);
```

How it works...

`Backbone.stickit` takes values for select list options from the `collection` property and assumes that it defines either a path to a collection relative to the window object or a function, which returns a collection. Also, an array of objects can be used instead of a collection, as shown in the previous example.

`labelPath` indicates a path to a property of a collection object, which is used as a label for select list options, and `valuePath` defines the path to an option value.

See also

▶ You can find additional details about binding a model and a collection to a select list on the `Bacbkone.stickit` **GitHub** page `http://nytimes.github.com/backbone.stickit/`

Handling keyboard shortcuts in a view

To perform the best user experience, your application should support various types of navigation within an application. One of these ways could be achieved by using shortcuts. Shortcut is a combination of keystrokes that provides easier access to a command or operation.

In this recipe, we are going to handle a couple of shortcuts for a view we implemented in the *Binding a collection to a view* recipe.

To perform keyboard shortcut handling, we are going to use the `Moustrap` library and the `Backbone.Mousetrap` extension, which provide the functionality we need.

Getting ready

You can download both the `Moustrap` library and the `Backbone.Moustrap` extension from the **GitHub** pages `https://github.com/ccampbell/mousetrap` and `https://github.com/elasticsales/backbone.mousetrap` respectively.

To include them into your project, save the `mousetrap.js` and `backbone.mousetrap.js` files into the `lib` folder and include references to them in `index.html`.

> Including a Backbone extension into your project is described in detail in the *Extending an application with plugins* recipe in *Chapter 1, Understanding Backbone*.

How to do it...

To perform keyboard shortcut handling, add the following property into a view object:

```
keyboardEvents: {
    'shift+n': 'addNewInvoiceItem',
    'shift+d': 'removeInvoiceItem',
},
```

How it works...

`Backbone.Mousetrap` automatically delegates keyboard events to a view when it's being created and undelegates when it is removed or when `undelegateEvents()` is called.

The following keys, `shift`, `ctrl`, `alt`, `option`, `meta`, and `command` are available. Other special keys are `backspace`, `tab`, `enter`, `return`, `capslock`, `esc`, `escape`, `space`, `pageup`, `pagedown`, `end`, `home`, `left`, `up`, `right`, `down`, `ins`, and `del`.

You should be able to reference any other key by names, such as a, /, $, *, or =.

By default, Mousetrap prevents shortcut events from being handled when the browser is focused on any form element, such as input, text area, or select box. However, if you want to handle a shortcut event for such elements, you can add the `mousetrap` class to it.

```
<textarea name="message" class="mousetrap"></textarea>
```

See also

> ▶ Please visit the following resource in order to learn more about Mousetrap: `http://craig.is/killing/mice`

Handling router events

Though there are not many use cases for handling router events, `Backbone.js` provides a mechanism to do so. In this recipe, we are going to create a simple application that logs router events.

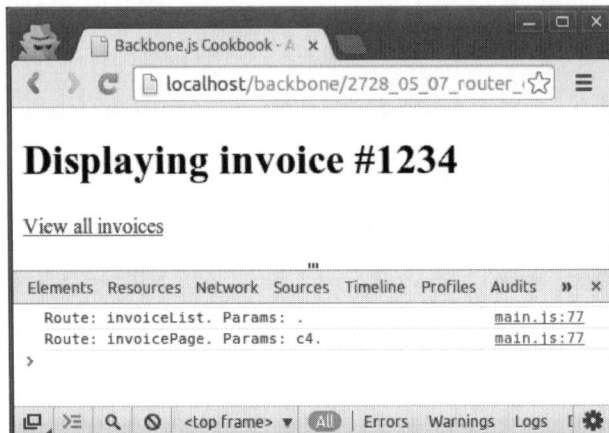

How to do it...

Perform the following steps in order to handle router events.

1. Listen to the `route` event of `Backbone.History`.

    ```
    initialize: function() {
      Backbone.history.on('route', this.routeTracker);
    },
    ```

2. Define the `route` event callback.

    ```
    routeTracker: function(router, route, params) {
      console.log(
        'Route: ' + route + '. Params: ' + params + '.'
      );
    },
    ```

How it works...

The `route` event is triggered after routing has been successfully performed. The `route` event callback accepts the following parameters:

- **router**: This parameter indicates a current router in use
- **route**: This parameter indicates a router callback name
- **params**: This indicates parameters passed to a router callback

There's more...

To handle a specific event for a specific router, listen to the `route:[name]` event.

```
var Workspace = Backbone.Router.extend({
  routes: {
    '': 'invoiceList',
    'invoice': 'invoiceList',
    'invoice/:id': 'invoicePage',
  },

  initialize: function() {
      this.on('route:invoicePage', this.invoicePageEvent);
  },

  invoicePageEvent: function(param1, param2) {
    console.log(param1);
  },
});
```

In this case, the event callback accepts the `routes` parameters.

See also

- More information about `routes` can be found in the *Implementing URL routing in your application* recipe in *Chapter 1, Understanding Backbone*

6

Templates and UX sugar

In this chapter, we will cover the following recipes:

- ▸ Using templates in a view
- ▸ Implementing a template loader
- ▸ Using Mustache templates
- ▸ Defining a form
- ▸ Adding validation to a form
- ▸ Handling form events
- ▸ Customizing a form with the Bootstrap framework
- ▸ Assembling layouts with LayoutManager
- ▸ Building a semantic and an easily styleable data grid
- ▸ Drawing on the HTML5 canvas

Introduction

This chapter introduces you to templates, which are used to separate HTML markup from the application code. Thus, the application becomes more structured and clean. We will discuss the templating engine provided by Underscore.js and learn how to integrate Backbone with third-party templating engines, such as Mustache.js.

Also, we will discuss useful Backbone extensions, which allows the use of forms, layouts, and grids.

Using templates in a view

In this recipe, you are going to learn how to use templates in the Backbone view. By default, Backbone.js is integrated with templating engine provided by Underscore.js.

Let's take an example of the *Rendering a collection in a view* recipe in *Chapter 4, Views*, where we rendered a collection with a view and updated the code using Underscore's templating engine. The result will look like the following image:

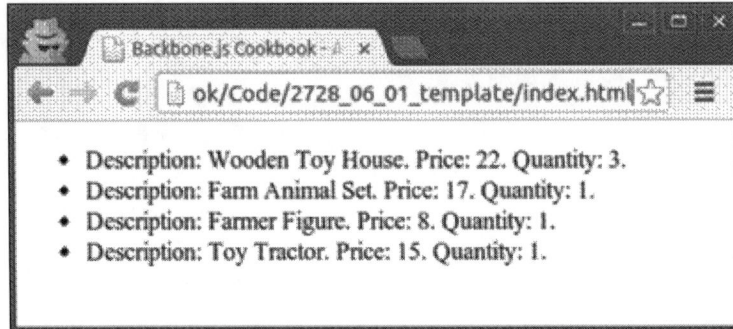

How to do it...

Follow these steps to use templates in a view:

1. Make sure you have models and collection objects defined.

   ```
   var InvoiceItemModel = Backbone.Model.extend({

   });

   var InvoiceItemCollection = Backbone.Collection.extend({
     model: InvoiceItemModel
   });
   ```

2. Define a view with the `template` property which contains a template. Then, when rendering a view, use `template()` to return rendered HTML.

   ```
   var InvoiceItemListView = Backbone.View.extend({

     // HTML element name, where to render a view.
     tagName: 'ul',
   ```

```
// Define template.
template: _.template(
   '<% _.each(items, function(item) { %>' +
   '   <li>' +
   '      Description: <%= item.description %>.' +
   '      Price: <%= item.price %>.' +
   '      Quantity: <%= item.quantity %>.' +
   '   </li>' +
   '<% }); %>'
),

// Render view.
render: function() {

   // Render template and set html for the view element
   // using jQuery.
   this.$el.html(this.template({
      items: this.collection.toJSON()
   }));

   return this;
   }
});
```

3. Create a collection instance.

```
var invoiceItemCollection = new InvoiceItemCollection([
   { description: 'Wooden Toy House', price: 22, quantity: 3 },
   {. description: 'Farm Animal Set', price: 17, quantity: 1 },
   { description: 'Farmer Figure', price: 8, quantity: 1 },
   { description: 'Toy Tractor', price: 15, quantity: 1 }
]);
```

4. Create a view instance, render it, and set the result to the value of body.

```
$('body').html(new InvoiceItemListView({
   collection: invoiceItemCollection
}).render().el);
```

How it works...

With the help of the _.template() method provided by Underscore.js, we can define an HTML template where we can include JavaScript code inside the <% ... %> brackets. To output a variable into the template, we need to use the <%= ... %> syntax, and to output an HTML escaped variable, we can use the <%- ... %> syntax.

Further, in the render() method, we pass the collection items in the JSON format into a template.

There's more...

In this section, we are going to learn how to split a template into partials.

Splitting a template into partials

Partial is a template that can be called from other templates as a function.

In case we want to reuse parts of the existing templates, we can split one template into different parts. To do so, follow these steps:

1. Define the template part.

```
itemTemplate: _.template(
  'Description: <%= description %>.' +
  'Price: <%= price %>.' +
  'Quantity: <%= quantity %>.'
),
```

2. Define the main template.

```
template: _.template(
  '<% _.each(items, function(item) { %>' +
  '  <li>' +
  '    <%= itemTemplate(item) %>' +
  '  </li>' +
  '<% }); %>'
),
```

3. When rendering a template, pass a partial method as a setting.

```
this.$el.html(this.template({
  items: this.collection.toJSON(),
  itemTemplate: this.itemTemplate
}));
```

See also

To get more information about templates in Underscore.js, you can refer to the official docs at http://underscorejs.org/#template.

Implementing a template loader

In a large application, which follows separation of concerned paradigm, it is important to store templates apart from views, so the web designer can modify them easily without harming views. Such a practice also provides template reusability within the application.

[
Store all your templates in a single HTML file

For server-side applications, developers typically store templates in separate files, achieving a convenient way for accessing and editing them. However, this can hardly be applied to client-side applications, because it makes a browser download multiple small files from a server, delaying an application start.
]

In this recipe we will store our templates apart from views in a single HTML file. Also, we will write a template loader, which will load those templates into the memory, allowing them to be accessed from all over the application.

How to do it...

Follow these steps to implement the template loader:

1. Add templates enclosed in the `script` tag to the header of the `index.html` file. Set the `id` attribute to distinguish one template from another.

```
<head>

    ...

    <script type="text/html" class="template" id="items">
      <% _.each(items, function(item) { %>
        <li>
          <%= itemTemplate(item) %>
        </li>
      <% }); %>
    </script>

    <script type="text/html" class="template" id="item">
      Description: <%= description %>.
      Price: <%= price %>.
      Quantity: <%= quantity %>
    </script>

</head>
```

2. Create a template loading utility and place it into the `js/template-loader.js` file.

```
(function ($) {

    $(document).ready(function () {

        // Store variable within global jQuery object.
        $.tpl = {}

        $('script.template').each(function(index) {

            // Load template from DOM.
            $.tpl[$(this).attr('id')] = _.template($(this).html());

            // Remove template from DOM.
            $(this).remove();
        });
    });

}) (jQuery);
```

3. Include the template loader into the `index.html` file.

```
<head>
    ...
    <script src="js/template-loader.js"></script>
    ...
</head>
```

4. When rendering a view, use templates defined in the global `$.tpl` array.

```
this.$el.html($.tpl['items']({
    items: this.collection.toJSON(),
    itemTemplate: $.tpl['item']
}));
```

How it works...

Because we defined our templates in `index.html`, they are loaded instantaneously. Then, in the template loader, when the document is fully loaded, we move them into the global variable `$.tpl` and remove templates from the DOM. This should speed up further usage of our templates as if we defined them in the JS file. Now, we can use those templates in different views of our application.

Using Mustache templates

Mustache is a beautiful, logicless template syntax. It can be used for HTML, config files, source code, and so on. There are various implementations of Mustache that exist for different languages, such as JavaScript, PHP, Ruby, Python, and many others.

In this chapter, we are going to learn how to use Mustache.js, which is the implementation of Mustache for JavaScript, with Backbone.js.

Getting ready

You can download Mustache.js from its GitHub page at `https://github.com/janl/mustache.js`. To include Mustache.js into your project, save the `mustache.js` file into the `lib` folder, and include a reference to it in `index.html`.

Including the Backbone extension into your project is described in detail in the *Extending an application with plugins* recipe in *Chapter 1, Understanding Backbone*.

How to do it...

Follow these steps to use a Mustache template:

1. Define a Mustache template in the view.

```
// Define template.
template: '{{#items}}<li>' +
          '  Description: {{description}}' +
          '  Price: {{price}}.' +
          '  Quantity: {{quantity}}.' +
          '</li>{{/items}}',
```

2. Run the `Mustache.render()` method to render a template.

```
this.$el.html(
  Mustache.render(this.template, {
    items: this.collection.toJSON()
  })
);
```

How it works...

`Mustache.render()` compiles a template string into a JavaScript code, and then executes it. A template string contains placeholders like `{{placeholder}}`, which are replaced with values provided in the second parameter.

There's more...

This section describes how to use compiled templates and partials in Mustache.js.

Using compiled templates

To improve the performance of your application, you can compile the template before using it by calling `Mustache.compile()`. This method accepts the template string as a single parameter and returns a JavaScript function, which can be called to return HTML code. The following example demonstrates how to do it:

```
var InvoiceItemListView = Backbone.View.extend({
  tagName: 'ul',

  template: Mustache.compile(
              '{{#items}}<li>' +
              '  Description: {{description}}' +
              '  Price: {{price}}.' +
              '  Quantity: {{quantity}}.' +
              '</li>{{/items}}'
            ),

  render: function() {
    this.$el.html(this.template({
      items: this.collection.toJSON()
    }));

    return this;
  }
});
```

Using partials

As in Underscore templates, Mustache.js allows partials to be used. To call a partial template, use the `>` syntax.

```
{{#items}}
  <li>{{> item }}</li>
{{/items}}
```

The partial template will look like this:

```
Description: {{description}}
Price: {{price}}.
Quantity: {{quantity}}.
```

You can pass the partial template in several ways, as follows:

- ▶ An object of partials, which are strings as well, may be passed as the third argument to `Mustache.render()`. The object should be keyed by the name of the partial, and its value should be the partial text.

```
Mustache.render(
  this.template,
  { items: this.collection.toJSON() },
  { item: this.itemTemplate }
);
```

- ▶ Template partials can also be compiled using the `Mustache.compilePartial()` function. The first parameter of this function is the name of the partial as it is named within a parent template. The second parameter is a partial template string.

```
Mustache.compilePartial(
  'item',
  'Description: {{description}}. Price: {{price}}.\
  Quantity: {{quantity}}.'
);
```

See also

To learn more about the Mustche.js syntax, you can visit its official GitHub page at `https://github.com/janl/mustache.js`.

Defining a form

Almost any web application requires an HTML form for user input. In the previous chapters, we learned how to render a form manually and bind it to the view model.

However, we should look for backbone-forms extensions, which allow us to deal with forms more easily by writing less code. In this recipe and in further recipes, we are going to learn how to use this extension.

Let's create a simple form for `BuyerModel`, which will look like the following screenshot:

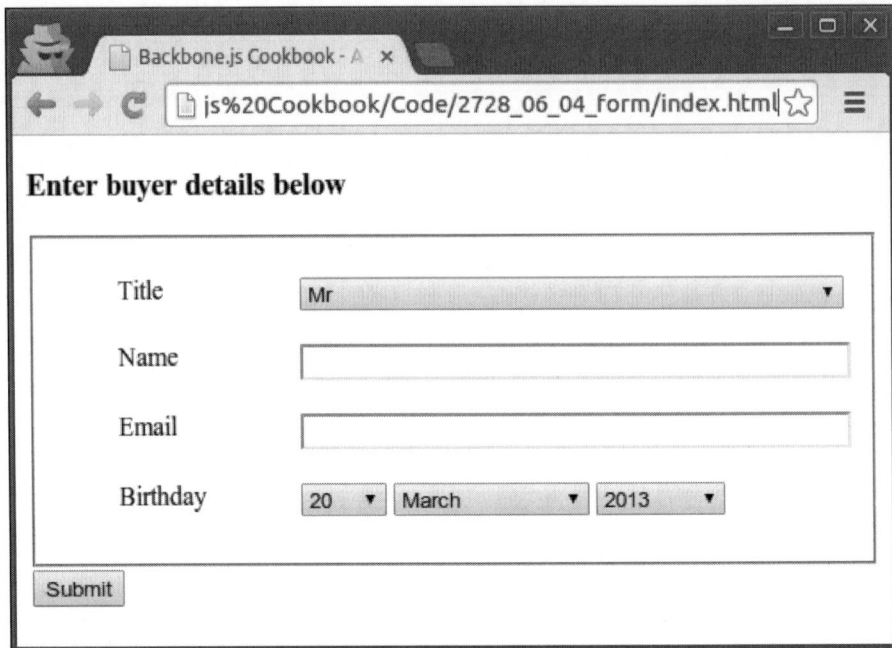

Getting ready

To include backbone-forms into your project, download the entire extension archive from the GitHub page (`https://github.com/powmedia/backbone-forms`), and extract it into the `lib/backbone-forms` directory. Then include a reference to the extension files into `index.html`.

```
<link href="lib/backbone-forms/distribution/templates/default.css"
rel="stylesheet" />

<script src="lib/backbone-forms/distribution/backbone-forms.min.js"></
script>
```

Including the Backbone extension into your project is described in detail in the *Extending an application with plugins* recipe in *Chapter 1, Understanding Backbone*.

How to do it...

Follow these steps to define a form:

1. Define a form schema definition inside the model object.

```
var BuyerModel = Backbone.Model.extend({
  schema: {
    title:    { type: 'Select', options: ['Mr', 'Mrs', 'Ms'] },
    name:     'Text',
    email:    { validators: ['required', 'email'] },
    birthday: 'Date',
  }
});
```

2. Create a view which should render a form with the help of the `Backbone.Form` object.

```
var BuyerFormView = Backbone.View.extend({
  render: function() {
    this.form = new Backbone.Form({ model: this.model });

    this.$el.html('<h3>Enter buyer details below</h3>');
    this.$el.append(this.form.render().el);
    this.$el.append('<button>Submit</button>');

    return this;
  },
});
```

3. Add a `submit` callback to the view. In this, the callback form is validated, and its values are passed to a model through the `commit()` method of the form.

```
events: {
  'click button': 'submit'
},

submit: function() {
  this.form.commit();

  console.log(this.model.toJSON());
  // Object { title: "Mr", name: "John Doe",
  // email: "john.doe@example.com",
  // birthday: Thu Mar 20 1986 00:00:00 GMT+0200 (EET) }
}
```

How it works...

The `Backbone.Form` object extends `Backbone.Views` by overriding the `render()` method, where it builds a form based on the schema definition we pass along with the model. If the model has initial values, then those values will be assigned to the form elements.

By executing the `commit()` method, form validation is performed and form values are assigned to the model properties. If the `{validate: true}` option is passed to this method, then both form validation and model validation are performed.

There's more...

This section describes how to build a form without a model.

Using a form without a model

We can create a form without tying a schema definition to a model. The following example shows how to do it:

```
var form = new Backbone.Form({
  data: {
    title: 'Mr',
    name: 'John Doe',
    email: 'john.doe@example.com',
    birthday: '1986-03-20'
  },

  schema: {
    title:    { type: 'Select', options: ['Mr', 'Mrs', 'Ms'] },
    name:     'Text',
    email:    { validators: ['required', 'email'] },
    birthday:'Date',
  }
}).render();
```

To get form values, use the `getValue()` method.

```
var this.data = this.getValue();
```

See also

To learn more about schema definition, you can check their official docs at
`https://github.com/powmedia/backbone-forms#schema-definition`.
In the later recipes, we will continue learning backbone-forms extension.

Adding validation to a form

In this recipe, we will continue to learn backbone-forms extension, and we will talk about form validation, which is quite a useful functionality and required by almost any web application which leverages backbone-forms extensions.

How to do it...

Follow these steps to add validation to a form:

1. Make sure you have model schema defined.

```
var BuyerModel = Backbone.Model.extend({
  schema: {
    email: 'Text',
  }
});
```

2. Add validators.

```
var BuyerModel = Backbone.Model.extend({
  schema: {
    email: {
      type: 'Text',
      validators: ['required', 'email']
    }
  }
});
```

3. Set a validation message.

```
var BuyerModel = Backbone.Model.extend({
  schema: {
    email: {
      type: 'Text',
      validators: [
        {
          type: 'required',
          message: 'Email field is required'
        },
        'email'
      ],
    }
  }
});
```

How it works...

To enable validation, we need to pass the `validators` array to a schema field definition. A validator can be a string, an object, a regexp (regular expression), or a function.

A string is used to set built-in validators, which do not require additional parameters. These validators are `required`, `email`, and `url`. If a validator requires an additional parameter (for example, `match` and `regexp`), or if we want to override an error message, we need to use an object to define a validator.

```
password: {
  validators: [ {
    type: 'match',
    field: 'passwordConfirm',
    message: 'Passwords must match!'
  }]
}
```

To perform a custom validator, we need to pass a validation function with two parameters: `value`, which is a form element value, and `formValues`, which is a hash of all form values.

```
//Custom function
username: { validators: [
  function checkUsername(value, formValues) {
    var err = {
      type: 'username',
      message: 'Usernames must be at least 3 characters long'
    };

    if (value.length < 3) return err;
  }
] }
```

Validation is performed when the `form.validate()` or `form.commit()` method is called.

There's more...

This section describes more about form validation.

Customizing error messages

It can be useful to override an error message for all built-in validators of a specific type at once. It is quite easy to do this by overriding values in `Backbone.Form.validators.errMessages` (the configuration object). We can use Mustache tags. Here is how it is done:

```
Backbone.Form.validators.errMessages.required =
  'Please enter a value for this field.';

Backbone.Form.validators.errMessages.match =
  'This value must match the value of {{field}}';

Backbone.Form.validators.errMessages.email =
  '{{value}} is an invalid email address.';
```

Performing a model validation

If you want to perform a model validation when committing or validating a form, you need to make sure that the model's `validate()` method returns an object of error messages keyed by the field names.

```
validate: function(attrs) {
  var errs = {};

  if (this.usernameTaken(attrs.username)) {
    errs.username = 'The username is taken'
  }

  if (!_.isEmpty(errs)) return errs;
},
```

See also

To learn more about form validation, you can refer to the docs at `https://github.com/powmedia/backbone-forms#validation`.

Handling form events

The `Backbone.Form` extension provides several events that we can use in our application. For example, by leveraging such events, we can implement specific functionalities where the value of one field depends on the value of another field.

In this recipe, we are going to create a form for the `InvoiceModel` model, where the **Paid Date** field will be shown only if the **Paid** option is selected as the **Status** field value. Our form will look like the following screenshot:

How to do it...

Follow these steps tohandle form events:

1. Define the model and the form schema.

```
var InvoiceModel = Backbone.Model.extend({
  schema: {
    referenceNumber: { type: 'Text'},

    date: { type: 'Date'},

    status: {
      type: 'Select',
      options: [
        { val: 'draft', label: 'Draft' },
```

```
                { val: 'issued', label: 'Issued' },
                { val: 'paid', label: 'Paid' },
                { val: 'canceled', label: 'Canceled' }
              ]
          }

        paidDate: { type: 'Date' },
      }
    });
```

2. Create `InvoiceForm` based on `Backbone.Form`.

    ```
    var InvoiceForm = Backbone.Form.extend({

    }
    ```

3. Override parent's `initialize()` method to bind the `status` field's `change` event to the callback, which will update dependent fields.

    ```
    initialize: function() {

        // Call parent method.
        InvoiceForm.__super__.initialize.apply(this, arguments);

        // Bind change status change event to the
        // update callback.
        this.on('status:change', this.update);
    }
    ```

4. Implement the `update` method for the form, which will update dependent fields.

    ```
    update: function(form, editor) {
        if (form.fields.status.editor.getValue() == 'paid') {
            form.fields.paidDate.$el.show();
        }
        else {
            form.fields.paidDate.$el.hide();
        }
    }
    ```

5. Override the `render` method of the form, where we need to run the `update` method to ensure dependent fields are shown properly.

    ```
    render: function() {

        // Call parent method.
        InvoiceForm.__super__.render.apply(this, arguments);
    ```

```
// Esnure dependent are shown properly.
this.update(this);

return this;
}
```

How it works...

`Backbone.Form` provides several form events, which we can bind to our callbacks using the `on()` method. They are:

- `change`: This event is triggered whenever something happens that affects the result of `form.getValue()`.

- `focus`: This event is triggered whenever this form gains focus, that is, when the input of an editor within this form becomes `document.activeElement`.

- `blur`: This event is triggered whenever this form loses focus, that is, when the input of an editor within this form stops being `document.activeElement`.

- `<key>:<event>`: the `change`, `focus`, or `blur` event is triggered for the form element specified by `key`.

`Backbone.Form` extends `Backbone.Views` and implements `initialize()` and `render()` methods. In our child object, we need to use these methods, and so we need to make sure parent methods are executed, which is possible because of JavaScript's `__super__` keyword. Then, apply the method.

See also

- The *Handling events of Backbone objects* recipe in *Chapter 5, Events and Bindings*

Customizing a form with the Bootstrap framework

Default backbone-form's styles look pretty boring, and we may want to replace them with something cool like Bootstrap. In this case, our form will look much better, as shown in the following screenshot:

Here we also use a List element (aka editor) to allow the user to input invoice item details. When user clicks on the **Add** button, the following popup is generated and shown to the user:

Getting ready

Follow these steps to be prepared to use Bootstrap.js:

1. Download the Bootstrap framework archive from its GitHub page at `http://twitter.github.com/bootstrap`, and extract it into the `lib` folder of the application.

2. Remove the `default.css` style's reference from `index.html`.

3. Include links to the Bootstrap files into `index.html`.

    ```html
    <link rel="stylesheet"
    href="lib/bootstrap/css/bootstrap.css" />

    <script src="lib/bootstrap/js/bootstrap.js"></script>
    ```

4. Include links to the `Backbone.Forms` extension, List editor, Bootstrap modal adapter, Bootstrap templates, and styles.

    ```html
    <script
    src="lib/backbone-forms/distribution/backbone-forms.js">
    </script>

    <script
    src="lib/backbone-forms/distribution/editors/list.js">
    </script>

    <script
    src="lib/backbone-forms/distribution/adapters/backbone.bootstrap-
    modal.js">
    </script>

    <script
    src="lib/backbone-forms/distribution/templates/bootstrap.js">
    </script>

    <link rel="stylesheet"
    href="lib/backbone-forms/distribution/templates/bootstrap.css" />
    ```

Including Backbone extension into your project is described in detail in the *Extending an application with plugins* recipe in *Chapter 1, Understanding Backbone*.

How to do it...

Follow these steps to customize a form with the Bootstrap framework:

1. Add the following line of code into `main.js` in order to set default modal adapter:

```
Backbone.Form.editors.List.Modal.ModalAdapter = Backbone.
BootstrapModal;
```

2. Add invoice items field definitions into the Backbone schema.

```
items:    {
    type: 'List', itemType: 'Object', subSchema: {
        description: { validators: ['required'] },
        price: 'Number',
        quantity: 'Number',
    }
}
```

How it works...

We included files which override default backbone-forms templates and styles in order to achieve integration with the Bootstrap framework. Also, we used List element, which makes a special call to the Bootstrap modal adapter to show a nice modal popup.

There's more...

This section describes how to override form templates.

Overriding form templates

In the previous example, we included `lib/backbone-forms/distribution/templates/bootstrap.js` into our project to make sure proper templates are used in order to provide integration with the Bootstrap engine. In this file, the `setTemplates()` method of the `Backbone.Form` object is called to override default templates.

```
var Form = Backbone.Form;

Form.setTemplates({
  form:
    '<form class="form-horizontal">{{fieldsets}}</form>',

  // ...
```

```
    field:
      '<div class="control-group field-{{key}}">' +
      '  <label class="control-label" for="{{id}}">' +
      '    {{title}}' +
      '  </label>' +
      '  <div class="controls">' +
      '    {{editor}}' +
      '    <div class="help-inline">{{error}}</div>' +
      '    <div class="help-block">{{help}}</div>' +
      '  </div>' +
      '</div>',
  }, {
    error: 'error'
    // Set error class on the field tag when validation fails
  });
```

Mustache syntax is used for template definition, and the templates that can be overridden are: `form`, `fieldset`, `field`, `nestedField`, `list`, `listItem`, `date`, `dateTime`, and `'list.Modal'`.

To use a specific template that is different from the one defined for the form element, add a template, and pass its name in the template parameter in the schema definition.

```
title: { type: 'Select', options: ['Mr', 'Mrs', 'Ms'], template:
'customField'}
```

To use a specific template for the form, pass its name when creating a new form.

```
this.form = new Backbone.Form({
  model: this.model, template: 'customForm'
});
```

See also

You can check the official Bootstrap.js docs to learn more about it at `http://twitter.github.com/bootstrap`. Also, look at the `lib/backbone-forms/distribution/templates/default.js` file to find out all the available templates which can be overridden.

Assembling layouts with LayoutManager

Backbone.LayoutManager is one of the most useful extensions for Backbone.js. It allows to build a layout out of panes easily and to get rid of many lines of code compared to using just Backbone views. LayoutManager also provides mechanisms to load templates from the main HTML file or external files.

Let's build an application which will have two panes. On the first pane, the user will see a list of invoices, and on the other pane he'll see invoice details.

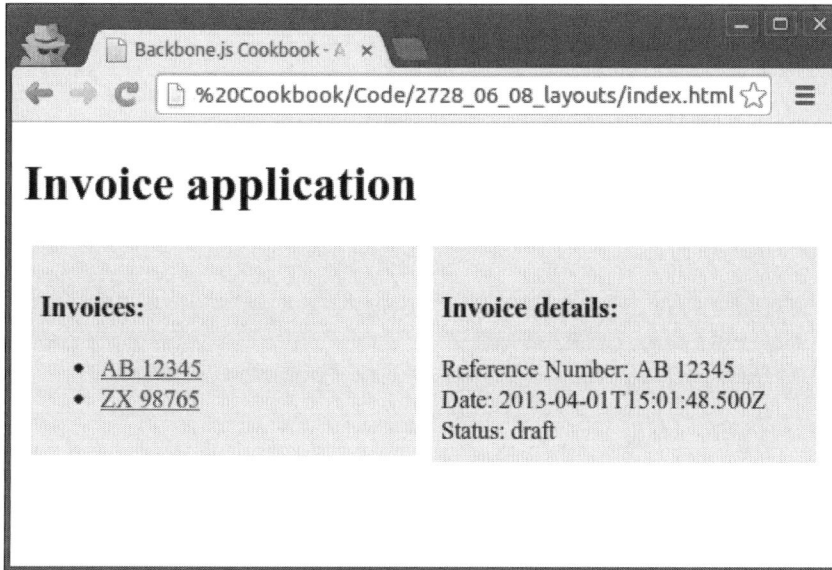

By clicking on the invoice number from the first pane, our application will update the second pane immediately.

Getting ready

You can download Backbone.LayoutManager from its GitHub page at `https://github.com/tbranyen/backbone.layoutmanager`. To include LayoutManager into your project, save the `backbone.layoutmanager.js` file into the `lib` folder and include a reference to it in `index.html`.

Including Backbone extension into your project is described in detail in the *Extending an application with plugins* recipe in *Chapter 1, Understanding Backbone*.

How to do it...

Follow these steps to assemble layouts:

1. Make sure you have model and collection objects defined.

```
var InvoiceModel = Backbone.Model.extend({

});

var InvoiceCollection = Backbone.Collection.extend({
  model: InvoiceModel
});
```

2. Define the invoice list pane.

```
var InvoiceListPane = Backbone.Layout.extend({

  // Returns selector for template.
  template: "#invoice-list-pane",

  // Set selector for template.
  serialize: function() {
    return {
      // Wrap the collection.
      invoices: _.chain(this.collection.models)
    };
  }
});
```

3. Define the invoice pane.

```
var InvoicePane = Backbone.Layout.extend({

  // Set selector for template.
  template: "#invoice-pane",

  // Returns data for template.
  serialize: function() {
    return {
      invoice: this.model
    };
  }
});
```

4. Define a router with routes and create the collection instance in its `initialize()` method.

```
var Workspace = Backbone.Router.extend({
  routes: {
    '': 'page',
    'invoice/:id': 'page',
  },

  // Initialize function run when Router object instance
  // is created.
  initialize: function() {
    //  Create collection
    this.collection = new InvoiceCollection([
      {
        referenceNumber: 'AB 12345',
        date: new Date().toISOString(),
        status: 'draft'
      },
      {
        referenceNumber: 'ZX 98765',
        date: new Date().toISOString(),
        status: 'issued'
      },
    ]);
  },

});
```

5. Add a page callback to the router, which creates a `Backbone.Layout` object and renders it.

```
page: function(id) {
  if (!id) {
    // Set default id.
    id = this.collection.at(0).cid;
  }


  var layout = new Backbone.Layout({
    // Attach the layout to the main container.
    el: "body",

    // Set template selector.
    template: "#layout",
```

```
          // Declaratively bind a nested View to the layout.
          views: {
            "#invoice-list-pane": new InvoiceListPane({
              collection: this.collection
            }),
            "#invoice-pane": new InvoicePane({
              model: this.collection.get(id)
            }),
          }
        });

        // Render the layout.
        layout.render();
      },
```

6. Add templates to the `<head>` tag of the page element.

```
<script class="template" type="template" id="layout">
  <h1>Invoice application</h1>
  <div id="invoice-list-pane"></div>
  <div id="invoice-pane"></div>
</script>

<script class="template"
    type="template"id="invoice-list-pane">
  <h3>Invoices:</h3>
  <ul>
    <% invoices.each(function(invoice) { %>
      <li>
        <a href="#invoice/<%= invoice.cid %>">
          <%= invoice.get('referenceNumber') %>
        </a>
      </li>
    <% }); %>
  </ul>
</script>

<script class="template" type="template" id="invoice-pane">
  <h3>Invoice details:</h3>
  Reference Number:
    <%= invoice.get('referenceNumber') %><br>
  Date: <%= invoice.get('date') %><br>
  Status: <%= invoice.get('status') %><br>
</script>
```

How it works...

The Backbone.LayoutManager object implements the template loader, the render() method, and provides many other cool features, which is typically done by the developer. In the views option, we can select which layout pane or Backbone view should be attached to the HTML elements that is specified in the main template for the layout.

See also

Please refer to the LayoutManager docs to learn more about the extension at https://github.com/tbranyen/backbone.layoutmanager/wiki.

Building a semantic and an easily styleable data grid

In your application, you may want to output the data as a sortable, filterable, and editable grid, which is not an easy task to do from scratch. In this recipe, we will learn a quick solution for that task using Backgrid.js, a powerful extension for building data grids in Backbone applications.

In this application, we are going to create a simple grid using the Backgrid example. It will look like the following screenshot:

When a user clicks on the column header, the grid is sorted by this column.

If a user double-clicks on a specific cell, that cell is replaced by an input element, where a user can enter a new value.

Getting ready

Follow these steps to be prepared to use Backgrid extension:

1. Download Backgrid.js extension from its official web site at `http://backgridjs.com/`.

2. Include Backgrid.js into your project by extracting this extension into the `lib/backgrid` folder.

3. Include references to the extension files into `index.html`.

```
<link rel="stylesheet"
href="lib/backgrid/lib/backgrid.css" />
<script src="lib/backgrid/lib/backgrid.js"></script>
```

Including Backbone extension into your project is described in detail in the *Extending an application with plugins* recipe in *Chapter 1, Understanding Backbone*.

How to do it...

Follow these steps to build a grid:

1. Make sure you have a model and collection objects defined.

    ```
    var InvoiceModel = Backbone.Model.extend({

    });

    var InvoiceCollection = Backbone.Collection.extend({
      model: InvoiceModel
    });
    ```

2. Create a collection instance.

    ```
    var invoiceCollection = new InvoiceCollection();
    ```

3. Define grid column settings.

    ```
    var columns = [
      {
        name: "referenceNumber",
        label: "Ref #",
        editable: false,
        cell: 'string'
      },
    ```

```
            {
              name: "date",
              label: "Date",
              cell: "date"
            },
            {
              name: "status",
              label: "Status",
              cell: Backgrid.SelectCell.extend({
                optionValues: [
                  ['Draft', 'draft'],
                  ['Issued', 'issued']
                ]
              })
            }
          ];
```

4. Initialize a new grid instance.

```
          var grid = new Backgrid.Grid({
            columns: columns,
            collection: invoiceCollection
          });

          $('body').append(grid.render().$el);

          invoiceCollection.add([
            {
              referenceNumber: 'AB 12345',
              date: new Date().toISOString(),
              status: 'draft'
            },
            {
              referenceNumber: 'ZX 98765',
              date: new Date().toISOString(),
              status: 'issued'
            },
          ]);
```

5. Add models into the collection.

```
          invoiceCollection.add([
            {
              referenceNumber: 'AB 12345',
```

```
            date: new Date().toISOString(),
            status: 'draft'
        },
        {
          referenceNumber: 'ZX 98765',
          date: new Date().toISOString(),
          status: 'issued'
        },
      ]);
```

6. Start the application.

```
    Backbone.history.start();
```

How it works...

`Backgrid.Grid` extends `Backbone.View` so you can create its instance and pass column settings keyed by the `columns` parameter. Column settings are defined as an array, and each row has the following properties:

 ▶ `name`: It's the name of the model property.

 ▶ `label`: It's the label of the heading column.

 ▶ `sortable`: It returns a boolean value to check whether a column is sortable.

 ▶ `editable`: It returns a boolean value to check whether a column is editable.

 ▶ `cell`: It's the cell type, which could be one of these: `datetime`, `date`, `time`, `number`, `integer`, `string`, `uri`, `email`, `boolean`, and `select`.

If you need to specify additional parameters for a cell type, you can extend the corresponding class and pass it to the `cell` property.

```
Backgrid.SelectCell.extend({
  optionValues: [
    ['Draft', 'draft'],
    ['Issued', 'issued']
  ]
})
```

There's more...

In this section, we are going to use several extensions for Backgrid, which can add extra features to our grid.

Performing bulk operations on grid models

We are going to add an extra column to our grid, which will contain checkboxes allowing users to select specific models in a grid and to perform bulk operations on them, for example, deleting. The following screenshot shows what our table will look like:

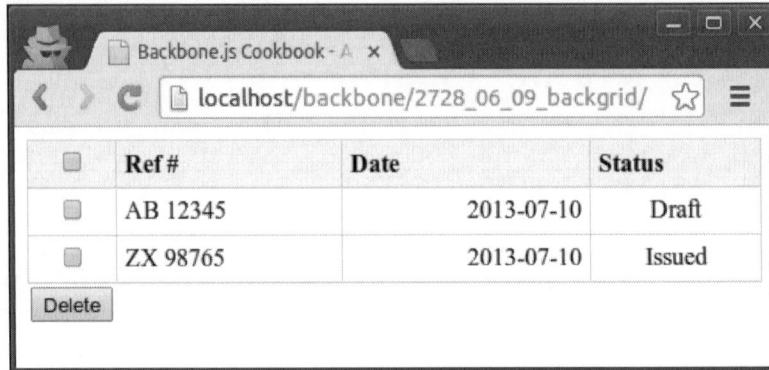

To complete this task, follow these steps:

1. Include the SelectAll extension files into `index.html`.

   ```
   <link rel="stylesheet" href="lib/backgrid/lib/extensions/select-
   all/backgrid-select-all.css" />

   <script src="lib/backgrid/lib/extensions/select-all/backgrid-
   select-all.js"></script>
   ```

2. Wrap grid into `TableView`.

   ```
   var TableView = Backbone.View.extend({
     initialize: function(columns, collection) {
       this.collection = collection;

       this.grid = new Backgrid.Grid({
         columns: columns,
         collection: this.collection
       });
     },

     render: function() {
       this.$el.html(this.grid.render().$el);

       return this;
     },
   });
   ```

3. Add the checkbox's column in the `initalize()` method.

```
initialize: function(columns, collection) {
  this.collection = collection;

  columns = [{
    name: "",
    cell: "select-row",
    headerCell: "select-all",
  }].concat(columns)

  this.grid = new Backgrid.Grid({
    columns: columns,
    collection: this.collection
  });
},
```

4. Append the delete button in the `render()` method.

```
render: function() {
  this.$el.html(this.grid.render().$el);

  this.$el.append('<button class="delete">Delete</button>');

  return this;
},
```

5. Handle the button click event.

```
events: {
  'click button.delete': 'delete'
},

delete: function() {
  _.each(this.grid.getSelectedModels(), function (model) {
    model.destroy();
  });
}
```

6. Create a new `TableView` instance and append it into the `body` element.

```
$('body').append(new TableView(columns, invoiceCollection).
render().$el);
```

Performing records filtering

To allow users to filter records, we are going to use the Select extension and the Lunr.js library, which is shipped with the Backgrid package. Also, we will apply Bootstrap styles to make the search box look neat.

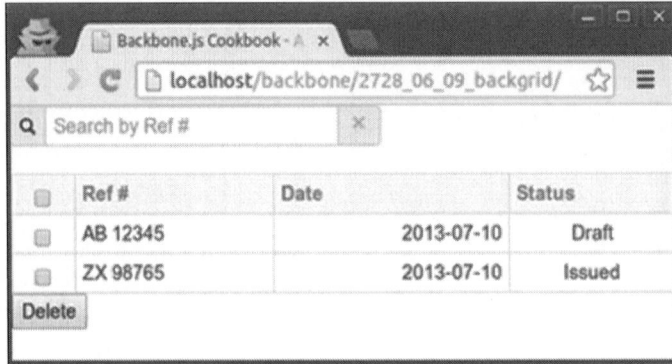

Follow these steps to perform records filtering:

1. Include Select extension, Lunr library, and Boostrap files into `index.html`.

   ```
   <link rel="stylesheet" href="lib/backgrid/assets/css/bootstrap.css" />

   <link rel="stylesheet" href="lib/backgrid/lib/extensions/filter/backgrid-filter.css" />

   <script src="lib/backgrid/assets/js/lunr.js"></script>

   <script src="lib/backgrid/lib/extensions/filter/backgrid-filter.js"></script>
   ```

2. Wrap grid into `TableView` as we did in the *Performing bulk operations on grid models* section.

3. Initialize `ClientSideFilter` in the `TableView.initalize()` method.

   ```
   this.clientSideFilter =
       new Backgrid.Extension.ClientSideFilter({
         collection: collection,
         placeholder: "Search by Ref #",
         fields: ['referenceNumber'],
         wait: 150
       });
   ```

4. Prepend the table with `ClientSideFilter` in the `TableView.render()` method.

```
this.$el.prepend(this.clientSideFilter.render().$el);
```

See also

Backgrid extension is actually very vast to be fully considered in this recipe. So, you can check the official Backgrid documentation at `http://backgridjs.com/`.

Drawing on the HTML5 canvas

Sometimes, we may want to render our view on the HTML5 canvas element, which can give more freedom and flexibility. The canvas can be used for rendering graphs as well as for creating an online game.

In this example, we are going to visualize the collection of models on the HTML5 canvas. The output of our code will look like the following screenshot:

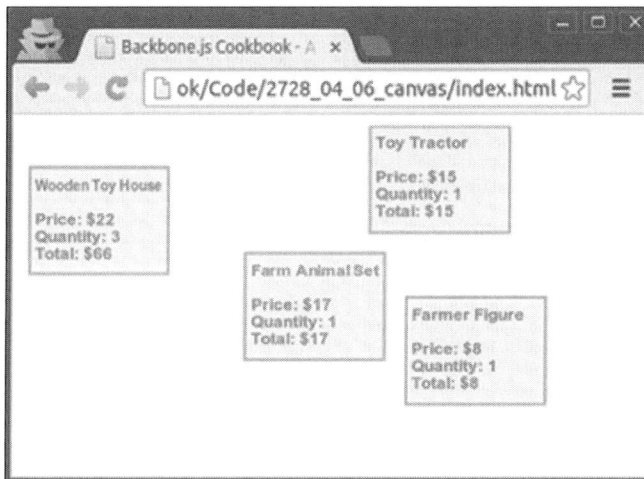

Getting ready

In this recipe, we are going to take an example from the *Splitting a view into subviews* recipe in *Chapter 4*, *Views*, to change `InvoiceItemView` and `InvoiceItemListView`.

How to do it...

Follow these steps:

```
InvoiceItemView  var InvoiceItemView = Backbone.View.extend({

});
```

1. Set box boundaries in the `initialize()` method of `InvoiceItemView`.

```
initialize: function() {
   // Set box size
   this.w = 100;
   this.h = 75;

   // Set random position
   this.x = Math.random() * (this.options.canvasW - this.w);
   this.y = Math.random() * (this.options.canvasH - this.h);
}
```

2. Draw a box and output model values on `ctx`, the canvas context, in the `render()` method of `InvoiceItemView`.

```
render: function() {

   // Get canvas context from parameters.
   ctx = this.options.ctx;

   // Draw transparent box
   ctx.fillStyle = '#FF9000';
   ctx.globalAlpha = 0.1;
   ctx.fillRect(this.x, this.y, this.w, this.h);

   // Stroke the box
   ctx.strokeStyle = '#FF9900';
   ctx.globalAlpha = 1;
   ctx.lineWidth = 2;
   ctx.strokeRect(this.x, this.y, this.w, this.h);

   // Output text in the box
   ctx.fillStyle = '#009966';
   ctx.font = 'bold 12px Arial';
   var textX = this.x + 4,
       textY = this.y + 4,
```

```
        textMaxW = this.w - 8,
        lineHeight = 12;

    ctx.fillText(
      this.model.get('description'),
      textX,textY + lineHeight, textMaxW
    );
    ctx.fillText(
      'Price: $' + this.model.get('price'),
      textX, textY + lineHeight*3,
      textMaxW
    );
    ctx.fillText(
      'Quantity: ' + this.model.get('quantity'),
       textX, textY + lineHeight*4, textMaxW
    );
    ctx.fillText(
      'Total: $' + this.model.calculateAmount(),
       textX, textY + lineHeight*5, textMaxW
    );

    return this;
  }
```

3. Define `InvoiceItemListView`, which creates an empty canvas and triggers model view rendering iteratively, passing `ctx` as an option.

```
var InvoiceItemListView = Backbone.View.extend({

  // Set a canvas as element tag name and define it's size.
  tagName: 'canvas',
  attributes: {
    width: 400,
    height: 200
  },

  // Render view.
  render: function() {

    // Get canvas context and it's size.
    var ctx = this.el.getContext("2d")
        canvasW = this.el.width,
        canvasH = this.el.height;
```

```
        // Clear canvas.
        ctx.clearRect(0, 0, canvasW, canvasH);

        // Iterate through models in collection and render them.
        this.collection.each(function(model) {
          new InvoiceItemView({
            model: model,

            // Pass canvas context and it's size.
            ctx: ctx,
            canvasW: canvasW,
            canvasH: canvasH
          }).render();
        }, this);

        return this;
      }
    });
```

How it works...

`InvoiceItemListView` defines canvas as a main view element and sets its boundaries. In the `render()` method, we get `ctx`, the context object of the canvas, by calling the `getContext()` method. Context object allows us to draw on the canvas by running special HTML5 methods.

By passing `ctx` and canvas dimensions to the subview as options, we allow them to be used for text and shapes output to the canvas.

See also

HTML 5 canvas reference could be found at
`http://www.w3schools.com/html/html5_canvas.asp`.

7

REST and Storage

In this chapter, we will cover the following recipes:

- ▶ Architecting the REST API for the backend
- ▶ Prototyping a RESTful backend with MongoLab
- ▶ Synchronizing models and collections with a RESTful service
- ▶ Building a RESTful frontend with Backbone
- ▶ Using the polling technique to fetch data
- ▶ Working with local storage

Introduction

This chapter focuses on the way Backbone.js synchronizes models and collections with a RESTful backend, or stores them in the HTML5 local storage.

We will learn how to design the REST API for our backend, which can be implemented with almost any programming framework, such as Symphony, Ruby on Rails, Django, or Node.js.

Throughout the chapter, we will use MongoLab (`http://mongolab.com`), which is the cloud version of MongoDB, with a RESTful interface. We will also learn what tools to use to debug the RESTful service when the frontend app has not been built yet.

Finally we will make the Backbone application communicate with the RESTful service, performing full set of CRUD operations supported by the REST server. We will also learn how to use the polling technique to update data in a collection in the application dynamically.

We will also discuss about an extension that allows us to keep data in HTML5's local storage instead of keeping them in the remote server.

Architecting the REST API for the backend

Representational State Transfer (**REST**) is an architectural style for designing network applications that communicate amongst each other. Unlike COBRA or SOAP, REST can be easily implemented on top of pure HTTP.

REST-style architectures consist of clients and servers. The client calls the HTTP request method (POST, GET, PUT, or DELETE) to perform CRUD (created, read, update, and delete) operation over a resource that can be either a collection or a single element.

In this recipe, we are going to architect an API of the REST server for the Billing application.

How to do it...

Follow these steps to architect an API of a RESTful service:

1. Define the base REST URI used by the client to access resources stored on the server; for example, it can look like http://example.com/resources.

2. Define URIs to access your app-specific resources. These URIs should be relative to the base REST URI:

   □ **Invoice collection**: <rest-uri>/invoices
   □ **Invoice**: <rest-uri>/invoices/<invoice-id>
   □ **Buyer collection**: <rest-uri>/buyers
   □ **Buyer**: <rest-uri>/buyers/<buyer-id>
   □ **Seller**: <rest-uri>/seller

How it works...

The URI to access the resource can look like http://example.com/resources/items and data, which are transferred through REST, and are typically in the JSON format, XML, or any other valid Internet media types.

The following table describes what happens when the REST operation is performed on a specific resource type:

Resource URI	Collection: http://example.com/ resources/items	Element: http://example.com/ resources/items/1
POST	This request creates a new item in the collection and returns a newly created item or its URI.	It's not typically used. If used, it does the same job as a POST query for a collection's resource.

GET	This request lists collection items or theirs URIs.	This request retrieves collection items by their URIs.
PUT	This request replaces the entire collection with another collection.	This request replaces collection items or creates one if it does not exist.
DELETE	This request deletes the entire collection.	This request deletes items from the collection.

Refer to the Roy Fieldings' PhD thesis, which is the first and most complete work about REST, to learn more about REST at `http://www.ics.uci.edu/~fielding/pubs/dissertation/rest_arch_style.htm`.

Prototyping a RESTful backend with MongoLab

Let's say we want to create a Backbone application that will communicate with a RESTful service. Should we start with creating a backend or a frontend? This question sounds like a dilemma, but the answer is very simple.

The easiest way is to create a prototype using a simple database with a REST-style interface, so we can quickly replace it with our own backend in the future.

There is a good tool for that named MongoLab (`http://mongolab.com`), which is the cloud version of MongoDB with a REST-style interface. MongoDB is a NoSQL document-oriented database that works with JSON-like data. MongoLab will not require us to write even a single line of code on the backend, so it is perfect for us as a prototyping tool.

To test and debug the MongoLab backend, we will use the Advanced REST client, which is an extension to the Chrome browser. It allows performing HTTP queries on a RESTful service and visualizes JSON data.

Getting ready...

Follow these steps to be prepared for this recipe:

1. Create an account on the MongoLab website (`https://mongolab.com`), or log in if you have an existing one.

2. Install the Advanced REST client on your browser using the URL `https://chrome.google.com/webstore/detail/advanced-rest-client/hgmloofddffdnphfgcellkdfbfbjeloo`. If you're using Firefox or Safari, you can easily find a similar extension for this purpose.

How to do it...

Follow these steps to create a MongoLab database and fill it with data:

1. Go to `https://mongolab.com/newdb` and create a new database named `billing-app` within your MongoLab account.

2. Go to `https://mongolab.com/user?username=<username>` and get an API key that you can use for authentication.

3. To check databases in your account, perform a GET request on a URI, say `https://api.mongolab.com/api/1/databases?apiKey=<your-api-key>`, using the Advanced REST client.

```
▶   https://api.mongolab.com/api/1/databases?apiKey=kNCrqJUqB4n1S_qW7wnXH43NH9XKjdlL
```

| ● GET | ○ POST | ○ PUT | ○ PATCH | ○ DELETE | ○ HEAD | ○ OPTIONS |

○ Other

| Raw | Form | **Headers** |

| Clear | Send |

The result will look like the following screenshot:

| Raw | JSON | **Response** |

Copy to clipboard   Save as file

```
[size(1)
  "billing-app"
]
```

4. To get a list of collections in the database, perform a `GET` request on the URI `https://api.mongolab.com/api/1/databases/billing-app/collections?apiKey=<your-api-key>`. The result will look like the following screenshot:

```
┌──────────────────────────────────────────────────────────────┐
│  ┌────────┐ ┌────────┐                                         │
│  │  Raw   │ │  JSON  │   Response                              │
│  └────────┘ └────────┘                                         │
│  ┌───────────────────────────────────────────────────────┐    │
│  │ Copy to clipboard  Save as file                        │    │
│  └───────────────────────────────────────────────────────┘    │
│  [size(2)                                                      │
│    "system.indexes",                                           │
│    "system.users"                                              │
│  ]                                                             │
│                                                                │
└──────────────────────────────────────────────────────────────┘
```

5. To create a new collection, let's send the collection items defined in the JSON format using a `POST` query on this URI: `https://api.mongolab.com/api/1/databases/billing-app/collections/invoices?apiKey=<your-api-key>`. Make sure that the **application/json Content-Type** header is set.

```
┌──────────────────────────────────────────────────────────────┐
│  ┌──────┐ ┌──────┐ ┌─────────┐                                 │
│  │ Raw  │ │ Form │ │ Files(0)│   Payload                       │
│  └──────┘ └──────┘ └─────────┘                                 │
│  Encode payload    Decode payload                              │
│     {                                                          │
│        referenceNumber: '98765',                               │
│        date: '2013-04-04',                                     │
│        items: [                                                │
│            { description: 'Jet Ski', price: 12, quantity: 1 }, │
│            { description: 'Toy Dolphin', price: 5, quantity: 1 }│
│                                                                │
│  ┌──────────────────────┐                                      │
│  │ application/json    ▼│  Set "Content-Type" header to overwrite this value. │
│  └──────────────────────┘                                      │
│                                    ┌───────┐   ┌───────┐       │
│                                    │ Clear │   │ Send  │       │
│                                    └───────┘   └───────┘       │
└──────────────────────────────────────────────────────────────┘
```

The result of such an operation will look like the following screenshot:

```
┌──────────────────────────────────────────────────────────────┐
│  ┌────────┐ ┌────────┐                                         │
│  │  Raw   │ │  JSON  │   Response                              │
│  └────────┘ └────────┘                                         │
│  ┌───────────────────────────────────────────────────────┐    │
│  │ Copy to clipboard  Save as file                        │    │
│  └───────────────────────────────────────────────────────┘    │
│  {                                                             │
│    "n": 2                                                      │
│  }                                                             │
│                                                                │
└──────────────────────────────────────────────────────────────┘
```

By performing a GET request on the same resource again, we will be returned inserted items with their IDs in the JSON format.

```
Raw        JSON        Response
Copy to clipboard   Save as file
[size(2)
 -{
   -"_id": {
      "$oid": "5163d7b5e4b0d2657f9860a7"
    },
    "referenceNumber": "12345",
    "date": "2013-04-02",
   -"items": [ ... size(2)]
  },
 -{
   -"_id": {
      "$oid": "5163d7b5e4b0d2657f9860a8"
    },
    "referenceNumber": "98765",
    "date": "2013-04-04",
   -"items": [ ... size(2)]
  }
]
```

6. To update an existing item in the collection, we need to perform a PUT request on the collection item resource, specified by its ID, in the URI https://api.mongolab. com/api/1/databases/billing-app/collections/invoices/<invoice- id>?apiKey=<your-api-key>. In the PUT request, we should pass an updated model in the JSON format. The result is also returned in JSON, as shown in the following screenshot:

```
Raw        JSON        Response
Copy to clipboard   Save as file
{
 -"_id": {
    "$oid": "5163d7b5e4b0d2657f9860a8"
  },
  "referenceNumber": "98765",
  "date": "2013-04-04",
 -"items": [size(2)
   -{
      "description": "Jet Ski",
      "price": 12,
      "quantity": 1
    },
   -{
      "description": "Toy Dolphin",
      "price": 5,
      "quantity": 1
    }
  ]
}
```

How it works...

MogoLab translates HTTP requests into MongoDB queries, which are executed, and the results are returned in the MongoDB Extended JSON format.

See also

▶ Refer to the MongoLab's REST API to learn more about performing queries at `https://support.mongolab.com/entries/20433053-REST-API-for-MongoDB`.

▶ You can also visit the following URL in order to meet specifications of the MongoDB Extended JSON format at `http://docs.mongodb.org/manual/reference/mongodb-extended-json/`

Synchronizing models and collections with a RESTful service

In this recipe, we are going to learn how to synchronize models and collections with a RESTful service. Just as we did in all other recipes, we will use MongoLab for a RESTful service.

How to do it...

Follow these steps to get familiar with REST in Backbone.js:

1. Create a configuration object that stores a server URL and an authentication key for MongoLab.

```
var appConfig = {
  baseURL: 'https://api.mongolab.com/api/1/databases/billing-app/
collections/',

  addURL: '?apiKey=kNCrqJUqB4n1S_qW7wnXH43NH9XKjdIL'
}
```

2. Define a `url()` method that returns a resource URL to perform a REST request. Such URLs should contain a model ID, if a model is already synchronized with a RESTful service. Also, such URLs should contain a MongoLab's authentication key.

```
var InvoiceModel = Backbone.Model.extend({
  url: function() {
    if (_.isUndefined(this.id)) {
      return appConfig.baseURL +
        'invoices' + appConfig.addURL;
    }
```

```
      else {
        return appConfig.baseURL + 'invoices/' +
          encodeURIComponent(this.id) + appConfig.addURL;
      }
    },
  });
```

Another way to do this is to define the `urlRoot` property, though it does not allow adding parameters to the URL.

```
var InvoiceModel = Backbone.Model.extend({
  urlRoot: appConfig.baseURL;
});
```

3. Define a new collection and a `url` property or `url()` method that should return the URL to a collection resource.

```
var InvoiceCollection = Backbone.Collection.extend({
  model: InvoiceModel,
  url: appConfig.baseURL +'invoices' + appConfig.addURL
});
```

4. To load data from a server into a collection, use the `fetch()` method. You can pass `success` and `error` callbacks as a parameter. Either of them will be called asynchronously if a synchronization succeeds or fails.

```
var collection = new InvoiceCollection();

collection.fetch({
  success: function(collection, response, options) {
    $('body').html(
      new View({ collection: collection}).render().el
    );
  },
  error: function(collection, response, options) {
    alert('error!');
  }
});
```

When the `fetch()` method is run, the read event is triggered. Also, on success, the sync event is triggered.

5. To load a specific model that exists on a server, you can also use the `fetch()` method, which works in a similar way as it worked for collection.

```
var model = new InvoieModel();

model.id = '5176396ce4b0c62bf3e53d79';
```

```
model.fetch(
    success: function(model, response, options) {
      // success
    },
    error: function(collection, response, options) {
      // error
    }
);
```

6. To sync a model with a RESTful service, use the `save()` method.

```
model.save();
```

To perform an update for a specific attribute , pass hash of changed attributes in the first parameter and `{patch: true}` in the second parameter.

```
model.save({ status: 'complete'}, {patch: true});
```

By default, the `save()` method works asynchronously, so you need to handle results in the `success` or `error` callbacks. However, if you need to run the `save()` method synchronously, pass `null` in the first parameter and `{wait: true}` in the second parameter.

```
model.save(null, {wait: true});
```

7. You can create a new model within a collection using the `create()` method. In this case, Backbone.js automatically calls the `save()` method and a new module is pushed to the server.

```
var model = collection.create(
    { referenceNumber: '123', status: complete },
    { wait: true }
);
```

8. You can destroy a model using the `destroy()` method, which removes a model both from a collection and a server.

```
model.save(null, {
    success: function(model, response, options) {
      // success
    },
    wait: true
});
```

How it works...

The `fetch()`, `save()`, or `destroy()` methods call the `sync()` method to perform HTTP queries to synchronize models and collections with a RESTful service. The `sync()` method accepts the following parameters:

- ▶ `method`: It can be either create, update, patch, delete, or read.
- ▶ `model`: It's either a model or a collection used to sync.
- ▶ `options`: These are the options accepted by the `$.ajax` variable.

You can override the `sync()` method if you need to override synchronization, or to use storage without a REST support.

There's more...

MongoLab returns data in the MongoDB Extended JSON format, which is not supported by Backbone.js by default. In this recipe, we are going to fix this and find a good solution to process MongoDB Extended JSON directly in a Backbone application.

Handling MongoDB Extended JSON

MongoLab (`http://mongolab.com`) is a RESTful service that transforms HTTP requests into MongoDB queries and returns the results in the MongoDB Extended JSON, which will look like the following code snippet:

```
{
    "_id": {
        "$oid": "516eb001e4b0799160e0e864"
    },
}
```

For appropriate results, we need to handle such IDs. The idea behind this is to override the `parse()` method, which processes JSON and initializes the model properties out of it. We are going to replace the format of an ID here:

```
Backbone.Model.prototype.parse = function(resp, options) {
    if (_.isObject(resp._id)) {
        resp[this.idAttribute] = resp._id.$oid;
        delete resp._id;
    }
    return resp;
},
```

Also, when the `sync()` method is run, we need to make sure that data is exported in the MongoDB Extended JSON format. In all the other cases, it should be exported in a regular JSON format. Data export is performed only in the `toJSON()` method, so we can do this by replacing the `toJSON()` method during the `sync()` method execution.

```
// Convert regular JSON into MongoDB extended one.

  Backbone.Model.prototype.toExtendedJSON= function() {
    var attrs = this.attributes;

    var attrs = _.omit(attrs, this.idAttribute);
    if (!_.isUndefined(this[this.idAttribute])) {
      attrs._id = { $oid: this[this.idAttribute] };
    }

    return attrs;
  },


// Substitute toJSON method when performing synchronization.

  Backbone.Model.prototype.sync = function() {
    var toJSON = this.toJSON;
    this.toJSON = this.toExtendedJSON;

    var ret = Backbone.sync.apply(this, arguments);

    this.toJSON = toJSON;

    return ret;
  }
```

See also

▸ The *Creating a Backbone.js extension with Grunt* recipe in *Chapter 8, Special Techniques*

▸ You may also be interested in checking the source code of `Backbone.sync` at `http://backbonejs.org/docs/backbone.html#section-134`.

▸ Visit the following URL in order to meet specifications of MongoDB Extended JSON at `http://docs.mongodb.org/manual/reference/mongodb-extended-json/`

Building a RESTful frontend with Backbone

In this recipe, we are going to write a frontend application that will act as a client for a RESTful service. For the backend, we will use the MongoLab service, which is a cloud version of MongoDB with a REST interface.

We will use the LayoutManager extension to output our views in a neat format. To build our application, we will take an example app from *Chapter 6, Templates and UX sugar*, and will modify it, so it will support data sync via REST and will look like the following screenshot:

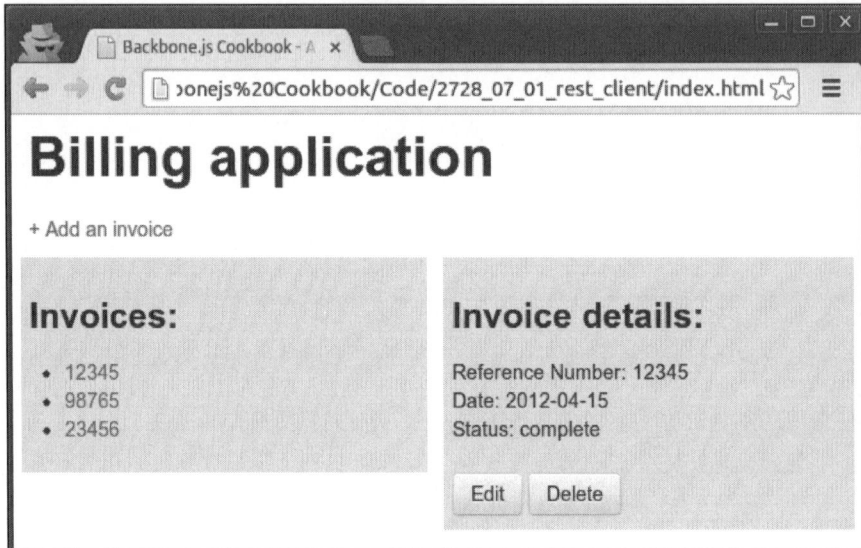

In the left-hand side pane, we can see a list of invoice titles, and in the right-hand side pane, we can see the invoice details. By default, these details are shown for the first invoice until the user clicks on a link in the left-hand side pane.

If the user clicks on the **Edit** button, the following form is shown:

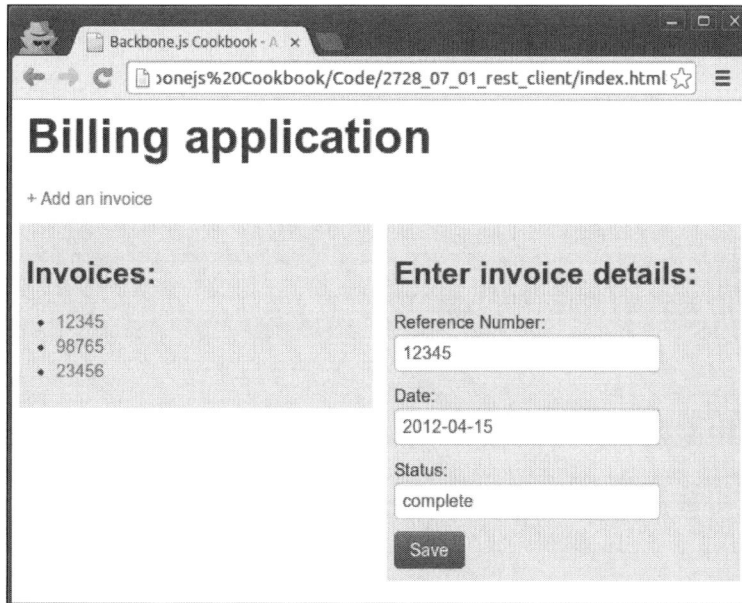

When the user clicks on the **Save** button, the model is updated, and it's JSON is sent to the server via REST, and the list in the left pane is also updated.

If the user clicks on the **Delete** button, a delete confirmation form appears, as shown in the following screenshot:

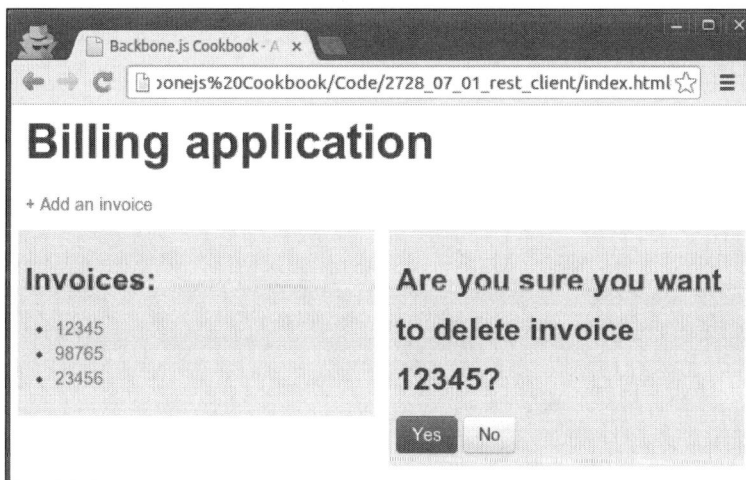

If the user confirms the deletion, the model is destroyed and removed from the server via REST.

Users can also create a new invoice by clicking on the **Add an invoice** link at the top of the page. Then, an Add Invoice form is shown, which is identical to the Edit form, with no data shown.

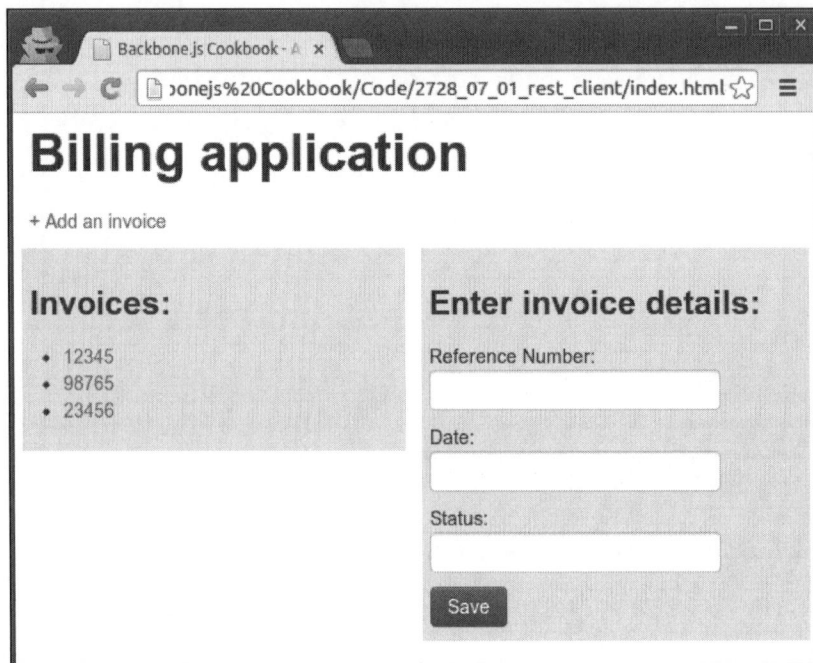

Getting ready...

Follow these steps to be prepared for this recipe:

1. Make sure the LayoutManager extension is installed. The usage and installation of this extension is described in the *Assembling layouts with LayoutManager* recipe in *Chapter 6, Templates and UX Sugar*.

2. Override `Backbone.Model` to support the MongoDB Extended JSON format, which is used in MongoLab.

```
// Convert MongoDB Extended JSON into regular JSON.
Backbone.Model.prototype.parse = function(resp, options) {
  if (_.isObject(resp._id)) {
    resp[this.idAttribute] = resp._id.$oid;
    delete resp._id;
  }
```

```
      return resp;
   },


   // Convert regular JSON into MongoDB extended one.
   Backbone.Model.prototype.toExtendedJSON= function() {
     var attrs = this.attributes;

     var attrs = _.omit(attrs, this.idAttribute);
     if (!_.isUndefined(this[this.idAttribute])) {
       attrs._id = { $oid: this[this.idAttribute] };
     }

     return attrs;
   },

   // Substute toJSON method when performing synchronization.
   Backbone.Model.prototype.sync = function() {
     var toJSON = this.toJSON;
     this.toJSON = this.toExtendedJSON;

     var ret = Backbone.sync.apply(this, arguments);

     this.toJSON = toJSON;

     return ret;
   }
```

This allows Backbone to work correctly with data IDs in a format like this:

```
{
    "_id": {
        "$oid": "516eb001e4b0799160e0e864"
    },
}
```

How to do it...

Follow these steps to create a RESTful application with Backbone:

1. Create a configuration object that we will store the server URL and authentication key.

```
var appConfig = {
  baseURL: 'https://api.mongolab.com/api/1/databases/billing-app/
collections/',

  addURL: '?apiKey=kNCrqJUqB4n1S_qW7wnXH43NH9XKjdIL'
}
```

2. Define `InvoiceModel` and set the `url()` method, which will return the model's resource URL to perform REST requests.

```
var InvoiceModel = Backbone.Model.extend({
  url: function() {
    if (_.isUndefined(this.id)) {
      return appConfig.baseURL +
        'invoices' + appConfig.addURL;
    }
    else {
      return appConfig.baseURL + 'invoices/' +
        encodeURIComponent(this.id) + appConfig.addURL;
    }
  },
});
```

3. Define `InvoiceCollection` and the `url()` method for the model.

```
var InvoiceCollection = Backbone.Collection.extend({
  model: InvoiceModel,
  url: function() {
    return appConfig.baseURL +
      'invoices' + appConfig.addURL;
  },
});
```

4. Define a router and add the `initialize()` method, which creates an empty collection and layout objects and renders a layout.

```
// Define router object.
var Workspace = Backbone.Router.extend({
  initialize: function() {

    //  Create collection.
    this.collection = new InvoiceCollection();

    // Create new layout.
    this.layout = new Backbone.Layout({
        // Attach the layout to the main container.
        el: 'body',

        // Set template selector.
        template: '#layout',

        // Declaratively bind a nested View to the layout.
        views: {
          '#first-pane': new InvoiceListPane({
```

```
            collection: this.collection
          }),
        },
      });

      // Render whole layout for the first time.
      this.layout.render();
    },
  });
```

5. Add a layout template into `index.html`.

```
<script class="template" type="template" id="layout">
  <h1>Billing application</h1>
  <div id="links-pane">
    <a href="#invoice/add">+ Add an invoice</a>
  </div>
  <div id="first-pane"></div>
  <div id="second-pane"></div>
</script>
```

6. Add `routes` and callbacks to the router object. Each callback calls the `switchPane()` method, which switches the right-hand side pane of the layout.

```
routes: {
  '': 'invoicePage',
  'invoice': 'invoicePage',
  'invoice/add': 'addInvoicePage',
  'invoice/:id/edit': 'editInvoicePage',
  'invoice/:id/delete': 'deleteInvoicePage',
  'invoice/:id': 'invoicePage',
},

// Page callbacks.
invoicePage: function(id) {
  this.switchPane('InvoicePane', id);
},
addInvoicePage: function() {
  this.switchPane('EditInvoicePane', null);
},
editInvoicePage: function(id) {
  this.switchPane('EditInvoicePane', id);
},
deleteInvoicePage: function(id) {
  this.switchPane('DeleteInvoicePane', id);
},
```

7. Add the `switchPane()` method to the router, which fetches collection from the RESTful service and switches the right-hand side pane.

```
switchPane: function(pane_name, id) {

    // Define panes array.
    // This will allow use to create new object from string.
    var panes = {
      InvoicePane: InvoicePane,
      EditInvoicePane: EditInvoicePane,
      DeleteInvoicePane: DeleteInvoicePane
    };

    // Update collection.
    this.collection.fetch({ success: function(collection) {

        // Get model by id or take first model
        // from collection.
        var model = _.isUndefined(id) ?
          collection.at(0) : collection.get(id);

        // Create new pane and pass model and collection.
        pane = new panes[pane_name] ({
          model: model, collection: collection
        });

        // Render pane.
        pane.render();

        // Switch views.
        window.workspace.layout.removeView('#second-pane');
        window.workspace.layout.setView('#second-pane', pane);

    }, reset: true });
  },
```

8. Define the invoice list pane.

```
var InvoiceListPane = Backbone.Layout.extend({

    // Returns selector for template.
    template: '#invoice-list-pane',

    // Set selector for template.
    serialize: function() {
      return { invoices: _.chain(this.collection.models) };
```

```
  },

  // Bind callbacks to collection event.
  initialize: function() {
    this.listenTo(this.collection, 'reset', this.render);
  }
});
```

Add a template for it in `index.html`.

```html
<script class="template" type="template" id="invoice-list-pane">
  <h3>Invoices:</h3>
  <ul>
    <% invoices.each(function(invoice) { %>
      <li>
        <a href="#invoice/<%= invoice.id %>">
          <%= invoice.get('referenceNumber') %>
        </a>
      </li>
    <% }); %>
  </ul>
</script>
```

9. Define a view invoice pane.

```
var InvoicePane = Backbone.Layout.extend({

  // Set selector for template.
  template: '#invoice-pane',

  // Returns data for template.
  serialize: function() {
    return { invoice: this.model };
  },

  // Bind callbacks to model events.
  initialize: function() {
    this.listenTo(this.model, 'change', this.render);
  }
});
```

Add a template for it in `index.html`.

```html
<script class="template" type="template" id="invoice-pane">
  <h3>Invoice details:</h3>
  Reference Number:
    <%= invoice.get('referenceNumber') %><br>
```

```
      Date: <%= invoice.get('date') %><br>
      Status: <%= invoice.get('status') %><br>
      <br>
      <a href="#invoice/<%= invoice.id %>/edit" class="btn">
        Edit
      </a>
      <a href="#invoice/<%= invoice.id %>/delete" class="btn">
        Delete
      </a>
    </script>
```

10. Define an edit invoice pane.

```
    var EditInvoicePane = Backbone.Layout.extend({

      // Set selector for template.
      template: '#edit-invoice-pane',

      // Returns data for template.
      serialize: function() {

        // Create new model if no model is given.
        return {
          invoice:
            _.isEmpty(this.model) ?
              new InvoiceModel() : this.model
        };
      },

      // Bind callbacks form events.
      events: {
        "click .submit": "save"
      },

      // Save model
      save: function() {
        var data = {
          referenceNumber:
            this.$el.find('.referenceNumber').val(),
          date: this.$el.find('.date').val(),
          status: this.$el.find('.status').val(),
        };

        var success = function(model, response, options) {
          window.workspace.navigate('#invoice/' + model.id, {
```

```
        trigger: true
      });
    };

    // Run appropriate method.
    if (_.isEmpty(this.model)) {
      this.collection.create(data, {success: success});
    }
    else {
      this.model.save(data, { success: success});
    }
  }
});
```

Add a template for it in `index.html`.

```
<script class="template" type="template"
    id="edit-invoice-pane">
  <h3>Enter invoice details:</h3>
  Reference Number:<br>
  <input class="referenceNumber" type="text"
      value="<%= invoice.get('referenceNumber') %>"><br>
  Date:<br>
  <input class="date" type="text"
      value="<%= invoice.get('date') %>"><br>
  Status:<br>
  <input class="status" type="text"
      value="<%= invoice.get('status') %>"><br>
  <button class="btn btn-primary submit">Save</button>
</script>
```

11. Define a delete invoice pane.

```
var DeleteInvoicePane = Backbone.Layout.extend({

  // Set selector for template.
  template: '#delete-invoice-pane',

  // Returns data for template.
  serialize: function() {
    return { invoice: this.model };
  },

  // Bind callbacks to form events.
  events: {
    "click .submit": "delete"
```

```
      },

      // Delete model.
      delete: function() {
        this.model.destroy({
          success: function(model, response) {
            window.workspace.navigate('#invoice', {
              trigger: true
            });
          }});
        }
    });
```

Add a template for it in `index.html`.

```html
<script class="template" type="template"
    id="delete-invoice-pane">
  <h3>Are you sure you want to delete invoice
  <%= invoice.get('referenceNumber') %>?</h3>
  <button class="btn submit btn-primary">Yes</button>
  <a href="#invoice/<%= invoice.id %>" class="btn">No</a>
</script>
```

12. Create a router instance and start the application.

```
    // Create the workspace.
    window.workspace = new Workspace();

    // Start the application.
    Backbone.history.start();
```

How it works...

To load the collection from a RESTful service, we need to call the `fetch()` method, which runs asynchronously as a regular AJAX call does. If we need to run any code after the data is fetched successfully, we need to pass the callback function in a second parameter keyed by the `success` key. If we need to perform a fallback behavior in case of an error, we should pass the callback function keyed by the `error` key in the function parameter.

```
collection.fetch({
  success: function(collection, response, options){
    // success behavior
  },

  error: function(collection, response, options){
    // fall back behavior
```

```
  }
})
```

To sync model with a remote server via REST, we use the `save()` method. To remove the model entirely from a remote server, we use the `destroy()` method. Both the methods accept the `success` and `error` callbacks.

See also

▸ The *Assembling layouts with LayoutManager* recipe in *Chapter 6, Templates and UX sugar*

▸ Refer to the official docs to get more information about Backbone methods we used in this recipe at `http://backbonejs.org/`.

Using the polling technique to fetch data

In the previous recipes, we were fetching data into a collection each time the router processed a URL change. We may wonder what happens if someone else updates data in the same storage? Can we see the updates immediately?

You might have seen how Facebook or Twitter updates a news feed in real time, and you may want to implement a similar behavior in your application. Typically, it can be done using the polling technique, which we are going to learn in this recipe.

We are going to create a web application that will update the collection view dynamically with the help of a polling technique.

Getting ready...

Override `Backbone.Model` and `Backbone.Collection` to support the MongoDB Extended JSON format, which is used in MongoLab.

```
// Convert MongoDB Extended JSON into regular JSON.
Backbone.Model.prototype.parse = function(resp, options) {
  if (_.isObject(resp._id)) {
    resp[this.idAttribute] = resp._id.$oid;
    delete resp._id;
  }

  return resp;
},


// Convert regular JSON into MongoDB extended one.
Backbone.Model.prototype.toExtendedJSON= function() {
```

```
      var attrs = this.attributes;

      var attrs = _.omit(attrs, this.idAttribute);
      if (!_.isUndefined(this[this.idAttribute])) {
        attrs._id = { $oid: this[this.idAttribute] };
      }

      return attrs;
    },

    // Substitute toJSON method when performing synchronization.
    Backbone.Model.prototype.sync = function() {
      var toJSON = this.toJSON;
      this.toJSON = this.toExtendedJSON;

      var ret = Backbone.sync.apply(this, arguments);

      this.toJSON = toJSON;

      return ret;
    }
```

How to do it...

Follow these steps to implement the polling technique:

1. Create a new polling collection that fetches data recursively and provides methods to start or stop polling.

```
var PollingCollection = Backbone.Collection.extend({
  polling: false,

  // Set default interval in seconds.
  interval: 1,

  // Make all object methods to work from its own context.
  initialize: function() {
    _.bindAll(this);
  },

  // Starts polling.
  startPolling: function(interval) {
    this.polling = true;

    if (interval) {
      this.interval = interval;
    }
```

```
        this.executePolling();
      },

      // Stops polling.
      stopPolling: function() {
        this.polling = false;
      },

      // Executes polling.
      executePolling: function() {
        this.fetch({
          success: this.onFetch, error: this.onFetch
        });
      },

      // Runs recursion.
      onFetch: function() {
        setTimeout(this.executePolling, 1000 * this.interval)
      },
    });
```

2. Define a configuration object.

```
    var appConfig = {
      baseURL:'https://api.mongolab.com/api/1/databases/billing-app/
collections/',
      addURL: '?apiKey=kNCrqJUqB4n1S_qW7wnXH43NH9XKjdIL'
    }
Define a model and a collection.
    var InvoiceModel = Backbone.Model.extend({
      url: function() {
        if (_.isUndefined(this.id)) {
          return appConfig.baseURL + 'invoices' +
            appConfig.addURL;
        }
        else {
          return appConfig.baseURL + 'invoices/' +
            encodeURIComponent(this.id) + appConfig.addURL;
        }
      },
    });


    var InvoiceCollection = PollingCollection.extend({
      model: InvoiceModel,
```

```
      url: function() {
        return appConfig.baseURL + 'invoices' +
          appConfig.addURL;
      },
    });
```

3. Define an invoice view and bind callbacks to model events.

```
    var InvoiceView = Backbone.View.extend({

      // Define element tag name.
      tagName: 'li',

      // Define template.
      template: _.template('Invoice #<%= referenceNumber %>.'),

      // Render view.
      render: function() {
        $(this.el).html(this.template(this.model.toJSON()));

        return this;
      },

      // Bind callback to the model events.
      initialize: function() {
        this.listenTo(this.model, 'change', this.render, this);
        this.listenTo(this.model, 'destroy', this.remove, this);
      }
    });
```

4. Define an invoice list view and bind callbacks to collection events.

```
    var InvoiceListView = Backbone.View.extend({

      // Define element tag name.
      tagName: 'ul',

      // Render view.
      render: function() {
        $(this.el).empty();

        // Append table  with a row.
        _.each(this.collection.models, function(model, key) {
          this.append(model);
        }, this);

        return this;
      },
```

```
    // Add invoice item row to the table.
    append: function(model) {
      $(this.el).append(
        new InvoiceView({ model: model }).render().el
      );
    },

    // Remove model from collection.
    remove: function(model) {
      model.trigger('destroy');
    },

    // Bind callbacks to the collection events.
    initialize: function() {
      this.listenTo(this.collection,'reset',this.render,this);
      this.listenTo(this.collection,'add',this.appen,this);
      this.listenTo(this.collection,'remove',this.remove,this);
    },
  });
```

5. Create a collection and render the corresponding view.

```
collection = new InvoiceCollection();

$('body').append('<h3>Invoices</h3>')
$('body').append(new InvoiceListView({
  collection: collection,
}).render().el);
```

6. Start polling.

```
collection.startPolling();
```

How it works...

The idea behind polling is to fetch the server regularly. However, we can't do this in a simple loop, because fetching works asynchronously, and we need to make sure AJAX requests do not overlap with each other. Thus, we need to make sure previous fetching is completed successfully before performing the next one.

In this recipe, we inherited a collection from `Backbone.Collection` and added new methods and properties that we needed to implement polling. In the `executePolling()` method, we are performing the `fetch()` method and passing the `onFetch()` method as a success callback. In the `onFetch()` method, we call the `executePolling()` method with a timeout.

Working with local storage

Sometimes, we need to store data on a browser storage rather than on a remote server. This is quite easy to do with the help of the Backbone extension known as localStorage Adapter, which overrides the behavior of the `Backbone.sync()` method to sync data with HTML5 local storage. In this recipe, we are going to learn how to use this extension.

Getting ready...

You can download the Backbone localStorage adapter from its GitHub page at `https://github.com/jeromegn/Backbone.localStorage`. To include this extension into your project, save the `backbone.localStorage.js` file into the `lib` folder and include a reference to it in `index.html`.

Including Backbone extension into your project is described in detail in the *Extending an application with plugins* recipe in *Chapter 1, Understanding Backbone*.

How to do it...

Extend the collection and set the `localStorage` key as follows:

```
var InvoiceCollection = Backbone.Collection.extend({
  model: InvoiceModel,

  // Use local storage.
  localStorage:
    new Backbone.LocalStorage("InvoiceCollection")
});
```

Here, we create an instance of `Backbone.LocalStorage` and pass the storage name as a constructor parameter. The storage name should be unique within your application.

How it works...

Backbone's localStorage adapter overrides the `Backbone.sync()` method, which executes a code to synchronize data with the HTML5 localStorage, if it is enabled for a collection.

> **Be aware when creating new models**
>
> The only thing you should avoid when using the localStorage adapter is creating new models and saving them by calling the `save()` method of the model. Instead, you should call the `create()` method of the collection object, because otherwise the model is not associated to a collection yet, and the localStorage adapter has no idea which local storage to use.
>
> After the model is associated with a collection, the `save()` method works pretty well.

See also

  ▸ There is also a Backbone extension that allows storing data in the WebSQL storage at `https://github.com/MarrLiss/backbone-websql`.

  ▸ There are plenty of extensions that allow using different storage engines at `https://github.com/documentcloud/backbone/wiki/Extensions,-Plugins,-Resources#storage`.

8
Special Techniques

In this chapter, we will cover:

- ▶ Using mixins with Backbone objects
- ▶ Creating a `Backbone.js` extension with Grunt
- ▶ Wiring tests for a Backbone extension with QUnit
- ▶ Mocking up a RESTful service with jQuery Mockjax in asynchronous tests
- ▶ Developing a mobile application with jQuery Mobile
- ▶ Building an iOS/Android app with PhoneGap
- ▶ Organizing a project structure with `Require.js`
- ▶ Ensuring compatibility with search engines
- ▶ Avoiding memory leaks in a Backbone application

Introduction

This chapter is aimed at showing how to solve the most challenging problems that can occur during Backbone development.

We are going to learn how to mix the existing Backbone objects to add any additional functionality. We will create a Backbone extension using Grunt.

We will also create tests for our extension, which will help us to ensure it works as expected when any new functionality is added to the extension.

Then, we will integrate **jQuery Mobile** and `Backbone.js` and will use **PhoneGap** to build native applications for mobile platforms such as iOS and Android.

We will learn how to deal with `Require.js`, how to use it to organize project structure, and how to use it in our mobile applications.

And finally, we will understand how to make the search engine index the AJAX application created with `Backbone.js`.

This chapter assumes that you are using a Unix like shell and have `Node.js` and npm (Node Package Modules) installed in your system.

Using mixins with Backbone objects

Though there are hundreds of Backbone extensions that provide additional functionality, a project may need to extend Backbone objects with some custom functionality.

There are several ways to do this. Typically, you can extend a Backbone object with the following code:

```
Backbone.ExtraModel = Backbone.Model.extend({
    // Add new method.
    hello: function() {

    },

    // Override existing method.
    toJSON: function() {

    }
});
```

It works great unless you face one of following scenarios:

▸ You want to modify the `Backbone.Model` object and all its children objects at once

▸ You have different extensions which together modify the same object, and thus you will need to avoid conflicts

The solution is to use mixins, which we are going to deal with within the scope of this recipe.

How to do it...

Perform the following steps to define `mixin` and add it to `Backbone.Model`:

1. Define the `mixin` object in the following way:

```
var mixin = {
    // Add new method.
    hello: function() {

    },
```

```
        // Override existing method.
        toJSON: function() {

        }
    }
```

2. Add `mixin` to the existing object as described in the following code:

```
Backbone.NewModel = Backbone.Model.extend(mixin);
```

3. Save `mixin` so that it can be mixed to the other model objects, if required.

```
Backbone.NewModel.mixin = mixin;
```

4. Another way is to apply mixin to `Backbone.Model.prototype`. This will make all `Backbone.Model` children to have such mixin.

```
_.extend(Backbone.Model.prototype, mixin);
```

5. If there are more functionalities you need to define them in different mixins, you can extend the Backbone object in a similar way:

```
_.extend(Backbone.Model.prototype, mixin2);
```

How it works...

To create a new model object, we used the `extend()` method provided by the ancestor model. To extend all Backbone models at once, we perform the mixing operation on the prototype of `Backbone.Model` using the `extend()` method of `Undercore.js`.

See also

▸ To understand prototype inheritance, please navigate to
   `http://en.wikipedia.org/wiki/Prototype-based_programming`

Creating a Backbone.js extension with Grunt

It could be very important for the developer to create a Backbone extension that will be shared with the rest of the world or even re used in future projects. In this recipe, we are going to learn how to create our own extension using Grunt, and we will upload it on **GitHub**.

Grunt is the JavaScript task runner that allows automating different tasks such as minification, compilation, unit testing, and linting. These repetitive tasks are defined in the `Gruntfile.js` file and are triggered from a console. There are many different packages for Grunt that are available as npm extensions. We are going to use one of them, named grunt-init, for scaffolding the Backbone extension from a template.

Our extension is going to provide a compatibility with MongoDB. In the previous chapter, we used MongoLab (`https://mongolab.com`), which is a MongoDB with a RESTful interface. **MongoLab** provides the data in the **MongoDB Extended JSON**, which is not supported by Backbone by default. The following code is an example of how a resource ID is presented in the MongoDB Extended JSON:

```
{
    "$oid": "<id>"
}
```

By default, the `Backbone.js` file does not deal with such IDs, but our extension will allow us to do this.

Getting ready...

Perform the following steps to get prepared for this recipe:

1. Make sure that `Node.js` and npm are installed.

2. Install `grunt-init`, which allows generating a project from a template.

   ```
   npm install -g grunt-init
   ```

3. Install `grunt-cli`, which allows running grunt commands from a command line.

   ```
   grunt-init-backbone-plugin npm install -g grunt-cli
   ```

4. Download `grunt-init-backbone-plugin` and place it in your local `grunt-init` directory.

   ```
   git clone --recursive https://github.com/dealancer/grunt-init-
   backbone-plugin.git ~/.grunt-init/backbone-plugin
   ```

5. Create the public repository on `http://github.com` where we will upload our extension.

How to do it...

Perform the following steps to create a Backbone extension with Grunt:

1. Create a directory that will contain the source code of our extension. This directory should be named `backbone-mongodb`.

   ```
   $ mkdir backbone-mongodb
   $ cd backbone-mongodb
   ```

2. Build an extension project from the Grunt template. Run the next command and follow the steps asked by Grunt.

   ```
   $ grunt-init backbone-plugin
   ```

3. Update the `backbone-mongodb.js` file with the following extension code:

```
// backbone-mongodb 0.1.0
//
// (c) 2013 Vadim Mirgorod
// Licensed under the MIT license.

(function(Backbone) {

  // Define mixing that we will use in our extension.
  var mixin = {

    // Convert MongoDB Extended JSON into regular one.
    parse: function(resp, options) {
      if (_.isObject(resp._id))  {
        resp[this.idAttribute] = resp._id.$oid;
        delete resp._id;
      }

      return resp;
    },

    // Convert regular JSON into MongoDB extended one.
    toExtendedJSON: function() {
      var attrs = this.attributes;

      var attrs = _.omit(attrs, this.idAttribute);
      if (!_.isUndefined(this[this.idAttribute]))  {
        attrs._id = { $oid: this[this.idAttribute] };
      }

      return attrs;
    },

    // Substitute toJSON method when performing synchronization.
    sync: function() {
      var toJSON = this.toJSON;
      this.toJSON = this.toExtendedJSON;

      var ret = Backbone.sync.apply(this, arguments);

      this.toJSON = toJSON;

      return ret;
    }
```

```
        }

        // Create new MongoModel object.
        Backbone.MongoModel = Backbone.Model.extend(mixin);

        // Provide mixin to extend Backbone.Model.
        Backbone.MongoModel.mixin = mixin;

        // Another way to perform mixin.
        //_.extend(Backbone.Model.prototype, mixin);

    }).call(this, Backbone);
```

4. Create the GitHub project by accessing the `https://github.com/new` link and fill the form that appears.

Owner   **Repository name**

🖼️ **dealancer** ▾ / `backbone-mongodb`   ✓

Great repository names are short and memorable. Need inspiration? How about **spawncamping-octo-meme**.

Description (optional)

Allows backbone models to work with MongoDB via REST.

◉ 📖 **Public**
      Anyone can see this repository. You choose who can commit.

◯ 🔒 **Private**
      You choose who can see and commit to this repository.

☐ **Initialize this repository with a README**
      This will allow you to `git clone` the repository immediately.

      Add .gitignore: **None** ▾

Create repository

5. Initialize the repository and push the code to the GitHub project.

```
$ git init
$ git remote add origin https://github.com/dealancer/backbone-
mongo.git
$ git add *
```

```
$ git add .gitignore
$ git commit -m "initial commit"
$ git push -u origin master
```

How it works...

When we run the `grunt-init` command with the `backbone-plugin` parameter, it builds a new project from the `backbone-plugin` template, which we downloaded and saved in the `~/.grunt-init/backbone-plugin` directory.

The newly generated project structure is as follows:

- `node_modules/`: This option provides Node.js modules for our application
  - `grunt/`
  - `grint-contrib-qunit/`
- `test/`: This option performs tests for our application
  - `index.html`
  - `mongodb.js`
- `vendor/`: This option lists the libraries used in the application
  - `backbone/`
- `backbone-mongodb.js`: This is the main file of our application
- `Gruntfile.js`: This is the Grunt file
- `LICENSE-MIT`
- `README.md`
- `package.json`: This is the Node.js module file

See also

- The source code of the extension is available at `https://github.com/dealancer/backbone-mongo`
- Grunt documentation is available at `http://gruntjs.com/getting-started`
- For more info about the `grunt-init` backbone plugin, please navigate to `https://github.com/gsamokovarov/grunt-init-backbone-plugin`

Writing tests for a Backbone extension with QUnit

If you are working on a complex project or a Backbone extension, you need to make sure that the new commits do not break any existing functionality. This is why many developers choose to create tests prior to or after writing new code.

For JavaScript applications, there are a good number of different testing tools that perfectly integrate with Backbone. In this recipe, we are going to learn one of the tools named QUnit.

When we were building our project from a template using Grunt, QUnit was included in the project, and the `test/mongodb.js` file was created. Let's add a simple test to the extension we did in the previous recipe.

How to do it...

Perform the following steps to test an application:

1. Edit the `test/mongodb.js` file and add some basic models and collections to the extension, as described in the following code:

```
var Book = Backbone.MongoModel.extend({
  urlRoot: '/books'
});

var Library = Backbone.Collection.extend({
  url: '/books',
  model: Book
});
```

2. Add some variables that we will use, as shown in the following code:

```
var library;

var attrs = {
    id: 5,
    title: "The Tempest",
    author: "Bill Shakespeare",
};
```

3. Add the `setup()` and `teardown()` methods, which will run before and after each test, as shown in the following code:

```
module('Backbone.Mongodb', _.extend(new Environment, {

  setup : function() {

    // Create new library.
```

```
library = new Library();

// Set init values.
library.create(attrs, {wait: false});
},

teardown: function() {

},
}));
```

4. Define as many tests as you need by calling the `test()` function as follows:

```
test("Export to MongoDB Extended JSON", 2, function() {
    var book = library.get(5);
    ok(book);

    var json = book.toJSON();
    equal(json._id.$oid, 5);
});
```

5. Run the tests by opening the `test/index.html` file in the browser, as shown in the following screenshot:

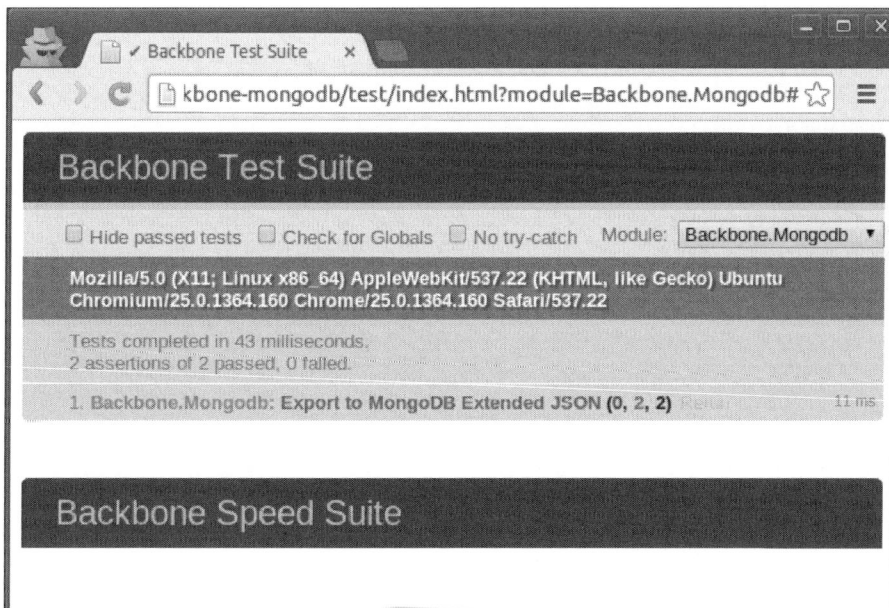

6. You can also run tests in a console with the following command, as shown in the following screenshot:

```
$ grunt
```

```
vadim@vjnotebook-tm:/var/www/backbone/2728_08_01_extension_and_tests/lib/backbone-mongodb$ grunt
Running "qunit:all" (qunit) task
Testing test/index.html...........................................................
..................................................................................
..................................................................................
....................MOCK GET: /books [object Object]
.MOCK GET: /books [object Object]
..OK
>> 759 assertions passed (6683ms)

Done, without errors.
vadim@vjnotebook-tm:/var/www/backbone/2728_08_01_extension_and_tests/lib/backbone-mongodb$ []
```

How it works...

QUnit runs all tests defined by the test() function, which takes the following parameters: name, amount of asserts, and callback function. Inside a testing callback, we can use the following asserts:

▸ ok(): This is a Boolean assertion that is equivalent to CommonJS's assert.ok() and JUnit's assertTrue(). It passes if the first argument is true.

▸ equal(): This is a non-strict comparison assertion that is roughly equivalent to JUnit assertEquals.

▸ notEqual(): This is a non-strict comparison assertion that checks for inequality.

▸ strictEqual(): This is a strict type and value comparison assertion.

▸ throws(): This is an assertion that tests if a callback throws an exception when run.

▸ notStrictEqual(): This is a non-strict comparison assertion that checks for inequality.

▸ deepEqual(): This is a deep, recursive comparison assertion that works on primitive types, arrays, objects, regular expressions, dates, and functions.

▸ notDeepEqual(): This is an inverted deep, recursive comparison assertion that works on primitive types, arrays, objects, regular expressions, dates, and functions.

If the required amount of asserts are achieved, the test is considered as successful.

Before running each test, QUnit runs the `setup()` function, and afterwards the `teardown()` function. This can be useful in case we need to change some global settings and then revert to the changes.

The Source code of the `index.html` file, which was generated by Grunt, looks like the following code:

```html
<!doctype html>
<html>
<head>
  <meta charset='utf8'>
  <title>Backbone Test Suite</title>
  <link rel="stylesheet"
    href="../vendor/backbone/test/vendor/qunit.css"
    type="text/css" media="screen">
  <script src="../vendor/backbone/test/vendor/json2.js">
  </script>
  <script src="../vendor/backbone/test/vendor/jquery.js">
  </script>
  <script src="../vendor/backbone/test/vendor/qunit.js">
  </script>
  <script src="../vendor/backbone/test/vendor/underscore.js">
  </script>
  <script src="../vendor/backbone/backbone.js"></script>
  <script src="../backbone-mongodb.js"></script>
  <script src="../vendor/backbone/test/environment.js">
  </script>
  <script src="../vendor/backbone/test/noconflict.js">
  </script>
  <script src="../vendor/backbone/test/events.js"></script>
  <script src="../vendor/backbone/test/model.js"></script>
  <script src="../vendor/backbone/test/collection.js">
  </script>
  <script src="../vendor/backbone/test/router.js"></script>
  <script src="../vendor/backbone/test/view.js"></script>
  <script src="../vendor/backbone/test/sync.js"></script>

  <script src="mongodb.js"></script>
</head>
<body>
  <div id="qunit"></div>
```

```
    <div id="qunit-fixture">
      <div id="testElement">
        <h1>Test</h1>
      </div>
    </div>
    <br>
    <br>
    <h1 id="qunit-header">
      <a href="#">Backbone Speed Suite</a>
    </h1>
    <div id="jslitmus_container" style="margin: 20px 10px;">
    </div>
  </body>
</html>
```

Also, the source code of the `Gruntfile.js` file, which describes the commands for Grunt, looks like the following code:

```
module.exports = function(grunt) {
  grunt.initConfig({
    qunit: {
      all: ['test/index.html']
    }
  });

  grunt.loadNpmTasks('grunt-contrib-qunit');

  grunt.registerTask('default', ['qunit']);
};
```

See also

▶ Please refer to the official QUnit documentation in order to get more familiar with it, at `http://api.qunitjs.com/`.

Mocking up a RESTful service with jQuery Mockjax in asynchronous tests

In the previous recipe, we got familiar with QUnit and tested the `toJSON()` method, which is used for pushing data to a RESTful service. In this recipe, we are going to test the `fetch()` method, which works asynchronously. Fortunately, QUnit allows us to create asynchronous tests. We also going to emulate a RESTful service using jQuery Mockjax.

Getting ready...

Download the jQuery Mockjax extension from its GitHub page, `https://github.com/appendto/jquery-mockjax`, and place it in the vendor directory of the extension. Then, include its main JS file in the `test/index.html` file.

```
<script src="../jquery-mockjax/jquery.mockjax.js"></script>
```

How to do it...

Perform the following steps to mock up a RESTful service for an asynchronous testing:

1. Define the mocked URLs and its output in the JSON format in the `setup()` method.

```
$.mockjax({
  url: '/books',
  responseTime: 10,
  responseText: [
    {_id: { "$oid": "10" }, one: 1},
    {id: "20", one: 1}
  ]
});

$.mockjax({
  url: '/books/10',
  responseTime: 10,
  responseText: {_id: { "$oid": "10" }, one: 1}
});

$.mockjax({
  url: '/books/20',
  responseTime: 10,
  responseText: {id: "20", one: 1}
});
```

2. Cancel mocking in the `teardown()` method.

```
$.mockjaxClear();
```

3. Add asynchronous tests that sync data from the mocked up RESTful service.

```
asyncTest("Read MongoDB Extended JSON", 1, function() {
  library.fetch();

  setTimeout(function() {
    ok(library.get('10'));
    start();
  }, 50);
});

asyncTest("Read regular JSON", 1, function() {
  library.fetch();

  setTimeout(function() {
    ok(library.get('20'));
    start();
  }, 50);
});
```

How it works...

In the previous code, we defined our test in the `asyncTest()` function, which works almost the same as the `test()` function, except that it does not proceed to the next test unless the `start()` function is called.

There is also a way to define asynchronous tests using the `test()` and `stop()` functions.

```
test("Read MongoDB Extended JSON", 1, function() {
  // do not proceed on the next stop unless start() is called
  stop();

  library.fetch();

  setTimeout(function() {
    ok(library.get('10'));
    start();
  }, 50);
});
```

From the previous code, we have seen that the `asyncTest()` function is an equivalent of the `test()` function, which calls the `stop()` function right away.

It is interesting to know what is happening in the mocked up service. jQuery Mockjax replaces the `jQuery.ajax()` method with its own method, which emulates AJAX calls to the server.

Mocked URLs are defined using `$.mockjax()` and canceled with some help from `$.mockjaxClear()`.

See also

▶ Please refer to the jQuery Mockjax documentation at
`https://github.com/appendto/jquery-mockjax`

▶ Docs about asynchronous testing with QUnit are available at
`http://api.qunitjs.com/category/async-control/`

Developing a mobile application with jQuery Mobile

jQuery Mobile is a useful HTML5/JavaScript framework for building mobile applications. It provides mobiles with look-and-feel components such as lists, buttons, toolbars, and dialogs. It is quite easy to create our own theme by customizing jQuery Mobile.

By default, all mobile pages can be stored in a single HTML file in different divs or are rendered on a fly. jQuery Mobile also allows us to use transition effects to switch between pages.

In this recipe, we are going to create a simple iOS-looking application with jQuery Mobile and `Backbone.js`, which allows users to view and create posts. Data is stored on `https://mongolab.com/welcome/` and accessed via REST.

Our application will look like the following screenshot:

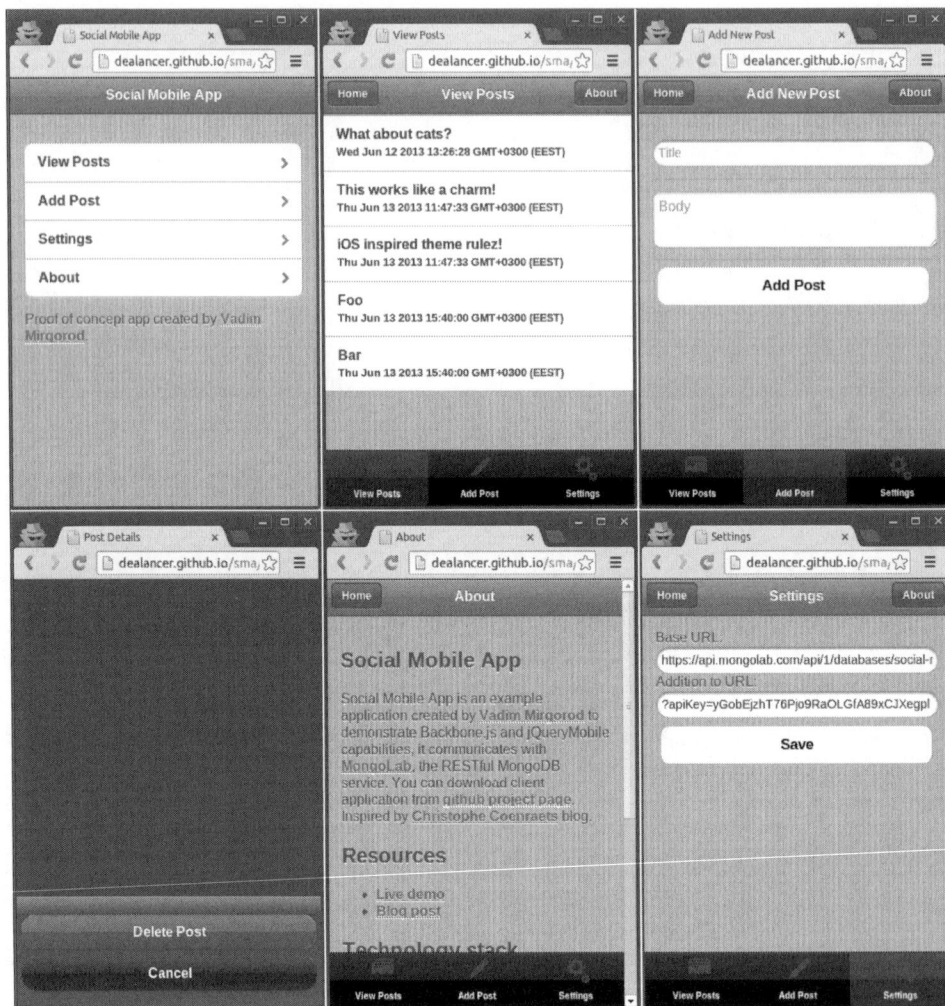

Getting ready...

Perform the following steps to get prepared for this recipe:

1. Download the backbone-mongodb extension from its GitHub page, `http://github.com/dealancer/backbone-mongodb/`, and save it in `lib/backbone-mongodb.js`. We are going to use backbone-mongodb to connect to `https://mongolab.com/welcome/`, the RESTful MongoDB service.

2. Download the jQuery Mobile library from `http://jquerymobile.com/` and extract it in the `lib/jquery.mobile/` folder.

3. Download the iOS-inspired theme for jQuery Mobile from its GitHub page, `https://github.com/taitems/iOS-Inspired-jQuery-Mobile-Theme`, and extract it in the `lib/ios_inspired/` folder.

4. Download the icons that we are going to use in our mobile app from `http://www.glyphish.com/`, and extract them into the `lib/glyphish/` folder.

How to do it...

Perform the following steps to create a mobile application:

1. Render a page in the mobile browser using the default browser width, otherwise the page could be rendered for 980 pixels screen width and then scaled down. Include the following line into the header of `index.html`:

   ```
   <meta name="viewport" content="width=device-width, initial-scale=1">
   ```

2. Include the CSS files into the header of `index.html`.

   ```
   <link rel="stylesheet" href="lib/jquery.mobile/jquery.mobile-1.1.0.min.css"/>
   <link rel="stylesheet" href="lib/ios_inspired/styles.css"/>
   <link rel="stylesheet" href="css/styles.css"/>
   ```

3. Create the `js/jqm-config.js` file that will retain the jQuery Mobile configuration and include this file it in `index.html`. Make sure it is included after jQuery and before jQuery Mobile.

4. Bind the callback to the `mobileinit` event in `js/jqm-config.js`.

   ```
   $(document).bind("mobileinit", function () {

   });
   ```

5. Disable the jQuery Mobile routing by adding the following code in the `mobileinit` event callback that we defined in the previous step:

   ```
   $.mobile.ajaxEnabled = false;
   $.mobile.linkBindingEnabled = false;
   $.mobile.hashListeningEnabled = false;
   $.mobile.pushStateEnabled = false;
   ```

6. Set up transitions and effects by adding the following code in the mobileinit event callback:

   ```
   $.extend($.mobile, {
     slideText: "slide",
     slideUpText: "slideup",
   ```

```
        defaultPageTransition: "slideup",
        defaultDialogTransition: "slideup"
    });
```

7. Remove the page from the **Document Object Model** (**DOM**) when it's being replaced. Add the following code into the mobileinit event callback:

```
$('div[data-role="page"]')
    .live('pagehide', function (event, ui) {
        $(event.currentTarget).remove();
    }
    );
```

8. Include the Backbone-mongodb extension in `index.html`.

```
<script src="lib/backbone-mongodb.js"></script>
```

9. Enable **Cross-site scripting** and disable the AJAX cache by adding the following code in `js/app-config.js`. Also, include this file in `index.html`. Make sure it is included before the main file of the application.

```
jQuery.support.cors = true;
jQuery.ajaxSetup({ cache: false });
```

10. Mix `Backbone.MongoModel` in `Backbone.Model` to support the MongoDB Extended JSON by adding the following command line in `js/app-config.js`:

```
_.extend(Backbone.Model.prototype,
Backbone.MongoModel.mixin);
```

11. Add the RESTful service URL in `js/app-config.js`.

```
var appConfig = {
    baseURL: 'https://api.mongolab.com/api/1/databases/social-
mobile-app/collections/',
    addURL: '?apiKey=yGobEjzhT76Pjo9RaOLGfA89xCJXegpl'
}
```

12. Add the template loader in `js/template-loader.js` and include this file in `index.html` before the main application file.

```
$(document).ready(function () {

    // Create global variable within jQuery object.
    $.tpl = {}

    $('script.template').each(function(index) {

        // Load template from DOM.
        $.tpl[$(this).attr('id')] = _.template($(this).html());
```

```
                    // Remove template from DOM.
                    $(this).remove();
                });

        });
```

13. Define the router object with routes and callbacks in `js/main.js`, which is our main application file. It should be included after all other files.

```
var Workspace = Backbone.Router.extend({
    routes: {
        "": "main",
        "post/list": "postList",
        "post/add": "postAdd",
        "post/details/:id": "postDetails",
        "post/delete/:id": "postDelete",
        "settings": "settings",
        "about": "about",
    },

    main: function() {
        this.changePage(new MainPageView());
    },

    postList: function() {
        var postList = new PostList();
        this.changePage(
            new PostListPageView({collection: postList})
        );
        postList.fetch();
    },

    postAdd: function() {
        this.changePage(new PostAddPageView());
    },

    postDetails: function(1d) {
        var post = new Post({id: id});
        this.changePage(new PostDetailsPageView({model: post}));
        post.fetch();
    },

    postDelete: function(id) {
        var post = new Post({id: id});
        this.showDialog(new PostDeleteDialogView({model: post}));
```

```
          post.fetch();
      },

      settings: function() {
        this.changePage(new SettingsPageView());
      },

      about: function() {
        this.changePage(new AboutPageView());
      }
    }
}
```

14. Add the `changePage()` method to the router object to switch to the current view page.

```
changePage: function (page) {
  $(page.el).attr('data-role', 'page');

  page.render();

  $('body').append($(page.el));

  $.mobile.changePage($(page.el), {
    changeHash: false,
    transition: this.historyCount++ ?
      $.mobile.defaultPageTransition : 'none',
  });
}
```

15. Add the `showDialog()` method to show dialogs in the router object.

```
showDialog: function(page) {
  $(page.el).attr('data-role', 'dialog');

  page.render();

  $('body').append($(page.el));

  $.mobile.changePage($(page.el), {
    allowSamePageTransition: true,
    reverse: false,
    changeHash: false,
    role: 'dialog',
    transition: this.historyCount++ ?
      $.mobile.defaultDialogTransition : 'none',
  });
},
```

16. Define the model and collection in `js/models/post.js` and include this file in `index.html`.

```
var Post = Backbone.Model.extend({
  defaults: {
    title: "",
    body: "",
    created: new Date().toString(),
  },

  url: function() {
    if (_.isUndefined(this.attributes.id)) {
      return appConfig.baseURL + 'posts' + appConfig.addURL;
    }
    else {
      return appConfig.baseURL + 'posts/' +
        encodeURIComponent(this.attributes.id) +
        appConfig.addURL;
    }
  },
});

var PostList = Backbone.Collection.extend({
  model: Post,
  url: function() {
    return appConfig.baseURL + 'posts' + appConfig.addURL;
  }
});
```

17. Define `PostDetailsView` and `PostDetailsPageView` in `js/views/post-details-page.js` and include this file in `index.html`.

```
var PostDetailsView = Backbone.View.extend({
  initialize: function() {
    this.model.bind('change', this.render, this);
    this.template = $.tpl['post-details'];
  },

  render: function() {
    $(this.el).html(this.template(this.model.toJSON())).
      trigger('create');
    return this;
  },
});
```

```
var PostDetailsPageView = Backbone.View.extend({
  initialize: function () {
    this.template = $.tpl['post-details-page'];
  },

  render: function (eventName) {
    $(this.el).html(this.template(this.model.toJSON()));
    this.postDetailsView = new PostDetailsView({
      el: $('.post-details', this.el), model: this.model
    });

    return this;
  }
});
```

18. Add templates for all your views in `index.html`. This will make them load faster. The following code is a template for the view we defined previously:

```
<script type="text/html" class="template"
        id="post-details-page">
  <div data-role="header">
    <h1>Post Details</h1>
    <a href="#post/list" data-rel="back" data-theme="a">
      Back
    </a>
    <a href="#about" data-theme="a">About</a>
  </div>

  <div data-role="content" class="post-details"></div>

  <div data-role="footer" data-position="fixed">
    <div data-role="navbar" data-theme="a">
      <ul>
        <li><a href="#post/list" id="list-button"
               data-icon="custom">
            View Posts
        </a></li>
        <li><a href="#post/add" id="add-button"
               data-icon="custom">
          Add Post</a></li>
        <li><a href="#settings" id="settings-button"
               data-icon="custom">
          Settings
        </a></li>
      </ul>
```

```
        </div>
      </div>
    </script>

    <script type="text/html" class="template" id="post-details">
      <h1><%= title %></h1>
      <small>Posted on <%= created %>.</small>
      <p><%= body %></p>

      <a href="#post/delete/<%= id %>" name="delete-post"
        id="delete-post" data-role="button">Delete Post
      </a>
    </script>

    <script type="text/html" class="template"
           id="post-list-item">
      <div class="ui-btn-inner ui-li">
        <div class="ui-btn-text">
          <a class="ui-link-inherit"
            href="#post/details/<%= id %>">
          <%= title %>
          <br><small><%= created %></small>
        </a>
      </div>
    </div>
  </script>
```

19. Add views and templates to show other pages.

20. Add styles in `index.html` to show the Glyphish icons at the bottom of the toolbar.

```
#list-button span.ui-icon-custom {
  background:
    url(../lib/glyphish/152-rolodex.png) 0 0 no-repeat;
}

#add-button span.ui-icon-custom {
  background:
    url(../lib/glyphish/187-pencil.png) 0 0 no-repeat;
}

#settings-button span.ui-icon-custom {
  background: url(../lib/glyphish/20-gear2.png) 0 0 no-repeat;
}
```

21. Check the order of CSS and JS inclusions in `index.html`. It should look like the following code:

```html
<!-- CSS -->
<link rel="stylesheet"
  href="lib/jquery.mobile/jquery.mobile-1.1.0.min.css"/>
<link rel="stylesheet" href="lib/ios_inspired/styles.css"/>
<link rel="stylesheet" href="css/styles.css"/>

<!-- Libraries -->
<script src="lib/jquery.min.js"></script>
<script src="js/jqm-config.js"></script>
<script src="lib/jquery.mobile/jquery.mobile-1.1.0.min.js">
</script>
<script src="lib/underscore-min.js"></script>
<script src="lib/backbone-min.js"></script>
<script src="lib/backbone-mongodb.js"></script>

<!-- Config -->
<script src="js/app-config.js"></script>

<!-- Template loader -->
<script src="js/template-loader.js"></script>

<!-- SMA models and views -->
<script src="js/model/post.js"></script>
<script src="js/view/post-list-page.js"></script>
<script src="js/view/post-add-page.js"></script>
<script src="js/view/post-details-page.js"></script>
<script src="js/view/post-delete-dialog.js"></script>
<script src="js/view/main-page.js"></script>
<script src="js/view/settings-page.js"></script>
<script src="js/view/about-page.js"></script>

<!-- SMA main file and router -->
<script src="js/main.js"></script>
```

How it works...

The main challenge of this recipe is to integrate jQuery Mobile with `Backbone.js`. Basically, there shouldn't be any problem unless you are trying to use the Backbone router. Both `Backbone.js` and jQuery Mobile provide their own routing mechanisms, which conflict with each other when used together.

The jQuery Mobile routing is enabled by default. You need to disable it manually if you want to use `Backbone.Router`. This is what we did in `js/jqm-comfig.js` in the previous section.

However, we still use jQuery Mobile to switch pages. To do this, we dynamically create a new page in the div and then call `$.mobile.changePage`, passing the new page element and other parameters. If transition effects are configured, animation is performed.

See also

▶ Please refer to the official jQuery Mobile resources:

  ❑ `http://view.jquerymobile.com/1.3.1/dist/demos/`

  ❑ `http://api.jquerymobile.com/`

▶ A live demo of the preceding application is available online at `http://dealancer.github.io/sma`. You can try it from your mobile device.

▶ The source code of this application is available in the GitHub repository: `https://github.com/dealancer/sma/`

Building an iOS/Android app with PhoneGap

PhoneGap is a free and open source framework that allows building mobile applications from HTML/CSS/JavaScript. It supports iOS, Android, Windows Phone, Blackberry, and some other mobile platforms. Also, developers can get access to the mobile device features, such as camera, contacts, geolocation, and storage.

To build a mobile application, you need to download a specific version of PhoneGap for the mobile platform with you are working. Also, there is a premium online service named **PhoneGap Build** that allows building mobile apps online. It integrates with GitHub and can extract recent version of the code.

In this recipe, we are going to build a mobile application with PhoneGap Build. It will be easy and cool.

Getting ready...

Please make sure you have created an account on the website `https://build.phonegap.com/apps`.

How to do it...

Perform the following steps to build an iOS/Android application with PhoneGap:

1. Create the `config.xml` file in the same directory where the `index.html` file is located.

2. Save the following PhoneGap configuration in the XML format in `config.xml`.

```xml
<?xml version="1.0" encoding="UTF-8" ?>
    <widget xmlns = "http://www.w3.org/ns/widgets"
        xmlns:gap = "http://phonegap.com/ns/1.0"
        id = "com.phonegap.example"
        versionCode ="1"
        version = "0.0.2">
    <!-- versionCode is optional and Android only -->

    <preference name="phonegap-version" value="2.7.0" />

    <name>Social Mobile App</name>

    <description>
      An example application to demonstrate Backbone.js and
      jQueryMobile capabilities.
    </description>

    <author href="http://vmirgorod.name"
        email="dealancer@gmail.com">
        Vadim Mirgorod
    </author>

    <icon src="icon.png" gap:role="default" />

    <preference name="orientation" value="portrait" />
</widget>
```

3. Place the `icon.png` file with the application icon in the root directory.

4. Go to `https://build.phonegap.com/apps/` and click on the **+ new app** button.

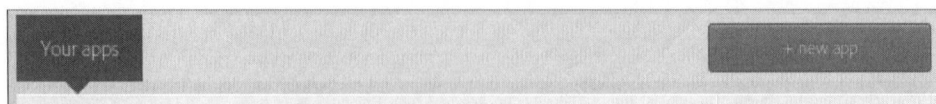

5. Enter the repository URL git://github.com/dealancer/sma.git in the form.

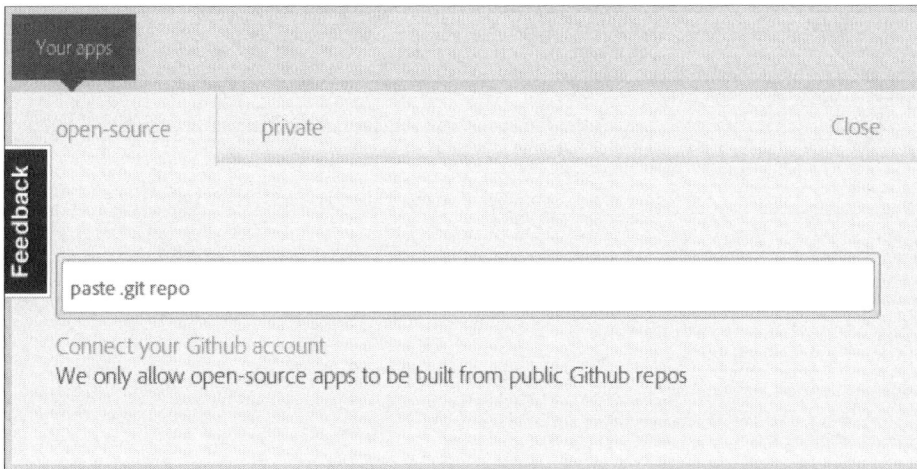

6. If you want to enter a non-GitHub account or upload an application from your machine, click on the **Private** tab. PhoneGap allows you to create one private application for free.

7. After the project is pulled out from the GitHub repository, click on the **Ready to Build** button, which launches the building process for multiple platforms. To build an application for iOS or Blackberry, you are required to enter a developer's key.

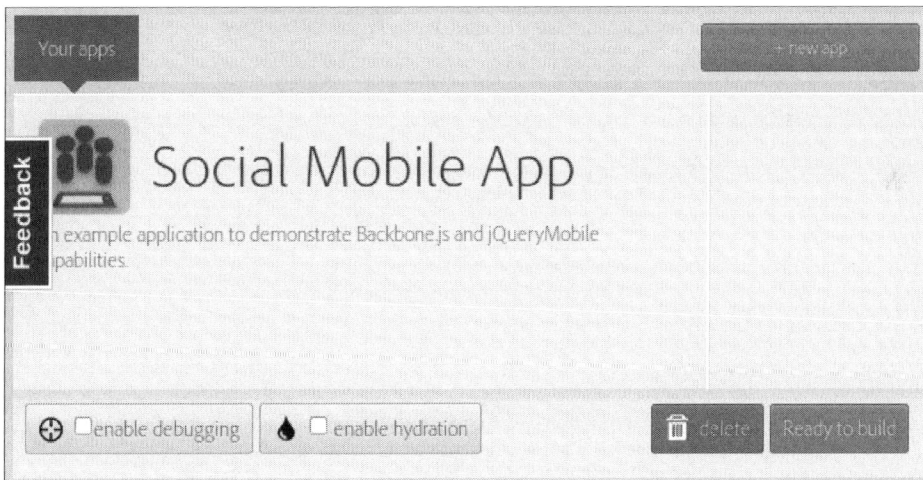

8. Now, the project is ready to be downloaded. You can do it by scanning the QR code on a mobile device. The QR code contains a link to your application. However, for many platforms, you need to place the built app on a special application market

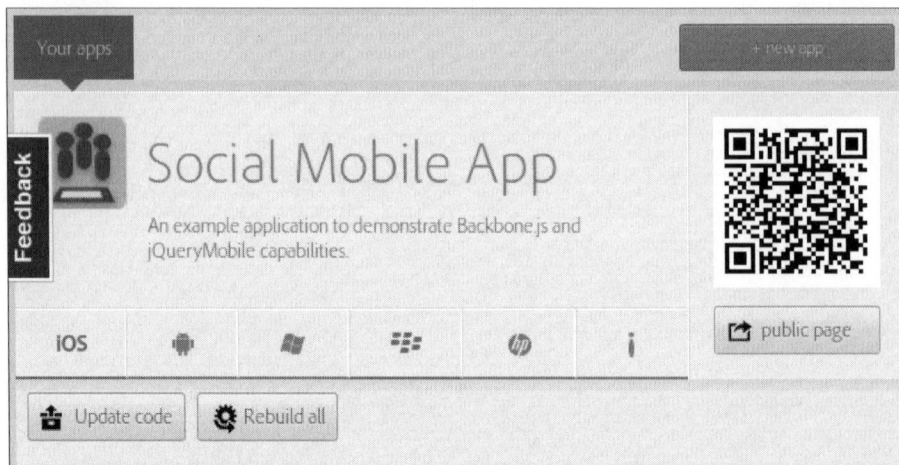

9. When you are ready to build a new version of the application, click on the **Update Code** button, and then click on the **Rebuild All** button.

See also

▶ Please refer to official PhoneGap docs at `http://docs.phonegap.com/en/edge/index.html`

Organizing a project structure with Require.js

In this recipe, we are going to use the **Asynchronous Module Definition** (**AMD**) technique that is implemented in `Require.js`, the JavaScript library, which helps to bring more order into your project. It allows you to define and load JavaScript modules dynamically from other parts of your code in a way similar to that in PHP using the `include` command. It can also optimize and uglify the JavaScript files so that they are loaded and executed faster.

We will take the **Social Mobile Application** example from the previous recipe and will refactor it using the `Require.js` library.

The directory structure of our app will look like the following structure:

▶ `css/`

  ❑ `main.css`

- ► js/
    - ❏ collection/
    - ❏ post.js
- ► model/
    - ❏ post.js
- ► view/
    - ❏ about-page.js
    - ❏ main-page.js
    - ❏ post-add-page.js
    - ❏ post-delete-dialog.js
    - ❏ post-details-page.js
    - ❏ post-list-page.js
    - ❏ settings-page.js
- ► app-config.js
- ► app.js
- ► jqm-config.js
- ► router.js
- ► template-loader.js
- ► lib/
    - ❏ glyphish/
    - ❏ ios_inspired/
    - ❏ jquery.mobile/
    - ❏ backbone-mongodb.js
    - ❏ backbone.js
    - ❏ jquery.js
    - ❏ require.js
    - ❏ underscore.js
- ► config.xml
- ► icon.png
- ► index.html
- ► README.md

Getting ready...

Download the `Require.js` file from `http://www.requirejs.org/docs/download.html`, and place it in the `lib` directory.

How to do it...

Perform the following steps to organize the mobile application with `Require.js`:

1. Extract the collection definition from `js/model/post.js` and place it in a separate file under the path `js/collection/post.js`.

2. Remove all CSS inclusions from the `index.html` file, and keep only a single one that should contain links to others.

```
@import url("../lib/jquery.mobile/jquery.mobile-1.1.0.min.css");
@import url("../lib/ios_inspired/styles.css");

// Custom styles
// ...
```

3. Remove all script inclusions from the `index.html` file and keep only the one that will load `Require.js`. Make sure to define the `data-main` attribute with a relative path to the main application file. No `.js` extension is required.

```
<script data-main="js/app"  src="lib/require.js"></script>
```

4. In the `js/app.js` file, add the `Require` configuration, which defines aliases to the libraries. We will use the other aliases later.

```
require.config({

  paths: {
    jquery            : '../lib/jquery',
    'jquery.mobile':
      '../lib/jquery.mobile/jquery.mobile-1.1.0',
    underscore: '../lib/underscore',
    backbone: '../lib/backbone',
    'backbone-mongodb': '../lib/backbone-mongodb',
  }

});
```

5. Define module dependencies by adding the shim property into the `Require` configuration.

```
shim: {
  'backbone-mongodb': {
    deps: ['backbone'],
```

```
    exports: 'Backbone'
  },
  'backbone': {
    deps: ['underscore', 'jquery'],
    exports: 'Backbone'
  },
  'underscore': {
    exports: '_'
  },
  'jquery.mobile': ['jquery','jqm-config'],
  'jqm-config': ['jquery'],
  'jquery': {
    exports: '$',
  }
}
```

Here we make Require know about third-party library dependencies; for example, `jquery.mobile` requires `jquery` and `jqm-config`, and should have been loaded earlier. If you use standard JS libraries with no AMD support, you should define objects that are provided by those libraries (for example,. `$` in jQuery). This can be done by defining the object name in the `export` property.

6. Add mapping settings into the `Require` configuration to load the `backbone-mongodb` object instead of the `backbone` object in all the JS files of your app; however, to load `backbone-mongodb`, we still need to load `backbone`.

```
map: {
  '*': {
    'backbone': 'backbone-mongodb',
  },
  'backbone-mongodb': {
    'backbone': 'backbone'
  }
}
```

7. Add the `requirejs()` function call to `js/app.js` to start an application. The first parameter contains an array of modules that should be loaded, while the second parameter provides the callback function, which is executed. Parameters of such callback functions are objects returned by the modules defined in the first parameter of the `requirejs()` function.

```
requirejs([ 'app-config', 'router' ],
function (appConfig, Router) {

  $(document).ready(function () {

    window.router = new Router();
```

```
         Backbone.history.start({ pushState : false });

      });

   });
```

The preceding code means that the `app-config.js` and `router.js` files will be included and implemented before executing the code in the callback function.

8. Refactor all your custom JS files to be AMD compatible. Add the `define()` function call, which has a similar syntax as the `requirejs()` function. If the module provides an object (or value) to be used by other modules, such an object should be returned by the module. The `app-config.js` file will look like the following code:

```
// Filename: app-config.js

define(['jquery', 'backbone'],
   function($, Backbone) {

      // Enable cross site scripting.
      $.support.cors = true;

      // Disable ajax cache.
      $.ajaxSetup({ cache: false });

      // Add support of MongoDB Extended JSON.
      _.extend(Backbone.Model.prototype,
         Backbone.MongoModel.mixin);

      // Return app configuration.
      return {
         baseURL: 'https://api.mongolab.com/api/1/databases/
            social-mobile-app/collections/',
         addURL: '?apiKey=yGobEjzhT76Pjo9RaOLGfA89xCJXegpl'
      }
   }
);
```

9. Though the `Require.js` file can load templates from the text files, let's deal with the template loader we used before. It also needs to be AMD compatible.

```
// Filename: template-loader.js

define(['jquery', 'underscore'],
   function($, _) {

      // Create global variable within jQuery object.
```

```
    var tpl = {};

    $('script.template').each(function(index) {

      // Load template from DOM.
      tpl[$(this).attr('id')] = _.template($(this).html());

      // Remove template from DOM.
      $(this).remove();
    });

    return tpl;
  }
);
```

10. Make sure all view files are refactored as well. They may look like the following code:

```
// Filename: about-page.js

define(['jquery', 'backbone', 'template-loader'],
  function($, Backbone, tpl) {
    return Backbone.View.extend({
      initialize: function () {
        this.template = tpl['about-page'];
      },

      render: function (eventName) {
        $(this.el).html(this.template());
        return this;
      },
    });
  }
);
```

11. Make sure all the required module dependencies are included in the `router.js` file.

```
// Filename: router.js

define([
  'jquery',
  'jquery.mobile',
  'backbone',
  'model/post',
  'collection/post',
  'view/about-page',
  'view/main-page',
```

```
        'view/post-add-page',
        'view/post-delete-dialog',
        'view/post-details-page',
        'view/post-list-page',
        'view/settings-page',
    ], function($, mobile, Backbone, PostModel, PostCollection,
        AboutPageView, MainPageView, PostAddPageView,
        PostDeleteDialogView, PostDetailsPageView,
        PostListPageView, SettingsPageView) {

    return Backbone.Router.extend({
       // Router code
    });
});
```

12. Remove the `main.js` file, because we have moved all functionality from it into the `app.js` and `router.js` files.

How it works...

The `Require.js` library provides two main functions, `define()` and `requirejs()`, to load other modules. The `requirejs()` function is used to start an application. Both the functions have similar syntax. The first parameter is used to list all the libraries required by the current module, and the second parameter contains the callback function that is executed.

```
define(['jquery', 'backbone', 'template-loader'],
    function($, Backbone, tpl) {

    return Backbone.View.extend({
       initialize: function () {
         this.template = tpl['about-page'];
       },

       render: function (eventName) {
         $(this.el).html(this.template());
         return this;
       },
     });
});
```

Parameters of the callback function are objects/values returned by the libraries required by the module. They are listed in the same order as the modules required.

If the module defines an object that is required by other modules, it should return such an object.

If you are dealing with no AMD library, but it provides an object to be used by other modules of your app, you should define such objects in the `require.config()` function.

```
require.config({
  shim: {
    'jquery': {
      exports: '$',
    }
  }
});
```

If you need to make sure that the modules are always loaded in a specific order, you should define the dependencies in the `require.config()` function.

```
require.config({
  shim: {
    'jquery.mobile': ['jquery','jqm-config'],
    'jqm-config': ['jquery'],
    'jquery': {
      exports: '$',
    }
  }
});
```

By default, the `Require.js` file loads a library using the path relative to the main project directory. The `.js` extension is used when referencing of such libraries is skipped. There is also a way to define path aliases in the `require.config()` function.

```
require.config({

  paths: {
    jquery            : '../lib/jquery',
    'jquery.mobile':
        '../lib/jquery.mobile/jquery.mobile-1.1.0',
  }

});
```

When the application is started, the main application file runs and all the required modules and libraries are loaded in the correct order and according to the definition and configuration.

There's more...

Optimizing JS files with r.js

R.js is a submodule of Require.js that can optimize JavaScript or CSS files by combining them into a single file and minimizing it so that it is loaded and executed much faster.

To load our Social Mobile Application from the localhost, it takes the browser to perform 27 requests, which is about 308 milliseconds.

Name Path	Me...	Status Text	Type	Initiator	Size Conte	Time Laten	Timeline 154 ms	231 ms	308 ms
/backbone/2728_	GET	OK	app...	Script	(fro...	0 ms			
jquery.mobile-1. /backbone/2728_	GET	200 OK	app...	require.js:1 Script	(fro...	0 ms 0 ms		◉	
tiling_stripes.gif /backbone/2728_	GET	200 OK	ima...	jquery.js:9(Script	(fro...	Pe...			◉
ajax-loader.gif /backbone/2728_	GET	200 OK	ima...	jquery.js:9(Script	(fro...	Pe...			◉
arrow_right.png /backbone/2728_	GET	200 OK	ima...	jquery.js:3: Script	(fro...	Pe...			◉

27 requests | 1.0 KB transferred | 308 ms (onload: 46 ms, DOMContentLoaded: 46 ms)

The same application, now optimized, is loaded with just 4 requests in 53 milliseconds.

Name Path	Me...	Status Text	Type	Initiator	Size Conte	Time Latency	Timeline 27 ms	40 ms	53 ms
index.html /backbone/2728_(	GET	304 Not M	text...	Other	212 B 7.5 KE	4 ms 3 ms	◉		
main.css /backbone/2728_(	GET	304 Not M	text...	index.html:! Parser	212 B 87.6 K	3 ms 3 ms		◉	
require.js /backbone/2728_(	GET	304 Not M	app...	index.html:1 Parser	212 B 16.4 K	5 ms 5 ms		◉	
app.js /backbone/2728_(	GET	304 Not M	app...	require.js:7 Script	212 B 226 KI	2 ms 2 ms			◉

4 requests | 848 B transferred | 53 ms (onload: 30 ms, DOMContentLoaded: 29 ms)

Here, we see a six times boost in performance, which is a good result. Actually, that boost could be even bigger for larger projects, which are loaded over slow Internet connection.

To optimize your app, please perform the following steps:

1. Make sure you have Node.js and npm installed.
2. Install Require.js as the Node module.

```
$ npm install -g requirejs
```

3. Create a new subdirectory named src and move all project files there.

4. Download `r.js` from `http://www.requirejs.org/docs/download.html` and save it into the root project directory.

5. Create the `app.build.js` file in the project root. This file should contain an `R.js` build configuration.

```
({
    appDir: "./src",
    baseUrl: "js",
    dir: "build",
    mainConfigFile: "src/js/app.js",
    modules: [
        {
            name: "app"
        },
    ]
})
```

6. Execute the following command to build the project:

```
$ node r.js -o app.built.js
```

You can find the built application in the `build` directory.

See also

▸ Check out the official `Require.js` documentation at `http://www.requirejs.org/`

Ensuring compatibility with search engines

When a search engine finds an AJAX-powered web application, it can't index such an app, because the search engine does not execute the complex JavaScript code. What the search engine wants is a static HTML.

In this recipe, we are going to learn how to make the search engine index the AJAX web application. We are going to deal mostly with Google, but we will also consider how to work with others.

The idea behind this recipe is that we can render the AJAX app into a static HTML page on the server and deliver it to a search engine spider via a proxy redirect.

To render JavaScript on the server, we are going to use the `Node.js` and `Phantom.js` files, which is a headless WebKit browser available as a Node module. We will also use a Node module named Seoserver that helps us to run `Phantom.js` and output the result.

To distinguish the search engine spider from a regular client and use a proxy redirect to the Seoserver, we will use Apache's `mod_rewrite`, `mod_proxy`, and `mod_proxy_http` modules.

Getting ready...

Perform the following steps to get prepared for this recipe:

1. Make sure you have `Node.js` and npm installed.

2. Install `Phantom.js` as a Node module.

   ```
   $ sudo npm install -g phantomjs
   ```

3. Install Seoserver, which is also a Node module.

   ```
   $ sudo npm install -g seoserver
   ```

4. Make sure you have Apache installed.

5. Make sure you have the following Apache extensions installed and configured: `mod_rewrite`, `mod_proxy`, and `mod_proxy_http`.

6. Make sure you have permissions to override a configuration in the `.htaccess` files.

How to do it...

Perform the following steps to ensure compatibility with search engines:

1. Tell **Google** bot to use `_escaped_fragement_` instead of `#!` by adding the following line into the header section of `index.html`.

   ```
   <meta name="fragment" content="!">
   ```

   We will learn what it means later.

2. Create the `.htaccess` file and place the following lines to perform the redirect operation via proxy to the Seoserver running on the 3000 port.

   ```
   <IfModule mod_rewrite.c>
    RewriteEngine on

    RewriteCond %{QUERY_STRING} ^_escaped_fragment_=(.*)$
    RewriteRule (.*) http://<host>:3000/<path>/index.html#%1? [P]
   </IfModule>
   ```

3. To redirect other search engines (for example, Yandex) to the Seoserver via proxy, add the following lines into the `.htaccess` file.

   ```
   RewriteCond %{HTTP_USER_AGENT} ^YandexBot
   RewriteRule (.*) http://<host>:3000/<path/>index.html#%1?
   ```

4. Start the Seoserver by running the following command.

   ```
   $ seoserver -p 3000 start > seoserver.log
   ```

5. Optionally, create a site map with URLs in the following format:
   `http://<host>/<path>index.html#!route`

6. You can check a result and see what the Google bot sees using the following link: `http://support.google.com/webmasters/bin/answer.py?hl=en&answer=158587`

> You can also check the result manually by accessing `http://<host>/<path>index.html?_escaped_fragment_=route`. In this case, make sure you have disabled JavaScript in your browser to avoid any conflicts.

How it works...

There is a way how **Googlebot** understands that the site supports the AJAX crawling scheme. It simply tries to access the website using URL like `http://<host>/</path>index.html#!route` and checks for any significant result. `#!` is used instead of `#` to indicate to the webmaster that it is exactly what Googlebot wants while trying to access the resource. Googlebot also scans the sitemap and tries to find URLs with the same URL scheme.

Webmaster should implement handling of such URLs and output the HTML snapshots that can be easily indexed by a search engine. In case if a URL with `#!` could not be processed by the server, it is allowed to use the following URL scheme: `http://<host>/</path>index.html?_escaped_fragment_=route`. This should be indicated by adding a special meta tag in the HTML output.

```
<meta name="fragment" content="!">
```

Such a URL scheme that is easily handled by Apache and Googlebot is redirected via the proxy to the server that outputs the HTML snapshot.

We will pass all parameters to the Seoserver, which is running on port 3000, and calls `phantom` to get the HTML snapshot of the requested resource.

Seoserver is written on `Node.js`. Let's see its sources in `seoserver.js`.

```
var express = require('express');
var app = express();
var arguments = process.argv.splice(2);
var port = arguments[0] !== 'undefined' ? arguments[0] : 3000;
var getContent = function(url, callback) {
  var content = '';
```

```
    var phantom = require('child_process').spawn(
      'phantomjs', [__dirname + '/phantom-server.js', url]
    );

    phantom.stdout.setEncoding('utf8');
    phantom.stdout.on('data', function(data) {
      content += data.toString();
    });

    phantom.stderr.on('data', function (data) {
      console.log('stderr: ' + data);
    });

    phantom.on('exit', function(code) {
      if (code !== 0) {
        console.log('We have an error');
      } else {
        callback(content);
      }
    });
  };

  var respond = function (req, res) {
    res.eader("Access-Control-Allow-Origin", "*");
    res.eader(
      "Access-Control-Allow-Headers", "X-Requested-With"
    );

    var url;
    if(req.headers.referer) {
      url = req.headers.referer;

    }
    if(req.headers['x-forwarded-host']) {
      url = 'http://' + req.headers['x-forwarded-host'] +
        req.params[0];

    };

    console.log('url:', url);

    getContent(url, function (content) {
      res.send(content);
    });
  }

  app.get(/(.*)/, respond);
  app.listen(port);
```

Seoserver also includes the `phantom-server.js` file with the following code:

```
var page = require('webpage').create();
var system = require('system');
var lastReceived = new Date().getTime();
var requestCount = 0;
var responseCount = 0;
var requestIds = [];

page.viewportSize = { width: 1024, height: 768 };

page.onResourceReceived = function (response) {
    if(requestIds.indexOf(response.id) !== -1) {
        lastReceived = new Date().getTime();
        responseCount++;
        requestIds[requestIds.indexOf(response.id)] = null;
    }
};

page.onResourceRequested = function (request) {
    if(requestIds.indexOf(request.id) === -1) {
        requestIds.push(request.id);
        requestCount++;
    }
};

page.open(system.args[1], function () {


});


var checkComplete = function () {
  if(new Date().getTime() - lastReceived > 300 && requestCount
      === responseCount)   {
    clearInterval(checkCompleteInterval);
    console.log(page.content);
    phantom.exit();
  } else {

  }
}
var checkCompleteInterval = setInterval(checkComplete, 1);
```

See also

▶ Check out the Seoserver source repository at
`https://github.com/apiengine/seoserver`

▶ To learn more about URL rewriting, please visit `http://publib.boulder.ibm.com/httpserv/manual60/misc/rewriteguide.html`

▶ The `Phantom.js` docs are available at
`https://github.com/ariya/phantomjs/wiki`

▶ Please refer to the Google Developers docs to learn more about AJAX app crawling at `https://developers.google.com/webmasters/ajax-crawling/`

Avoiding memory leaks in a Backbone application

A memory leak is a problem that can occur in a computer program due to incorrect memory allocation. In high-level object-oriented languages such as JavaScript, memory leak is often related to an object that is stored in the memory but isn't used by an application code. A memory leak can lead to a more serious problem such as exhausting the available system memory.

The following example demonstrates memory leak caused by a closure (anonymous function):

```
var div = document.createElement("div");
div.onclick = function () {   }
```

In the preceding code, a new HTML element is created and the `onclick` callback is assigned to an anonymous function. Such a code produces a memory leak because `div` references to a closure, while closure references to a div since the div variable can be accessed in a closure scope. Such cyclic referencing can produce a memory leak because neither div nor closure is utilized by a garbage collector.

In this recipe, we will learn how to detect memory leaks in a Backbone application and how to fix them. We will use Google Chrome Heap Profiler, which is a part of the Google Chrome browser.

Getting ready...

In this recipe, we are going to take an example application from the recipe binding a collection to a view of *Chapter 5, Events and Binding* and modify it. Such modifications are not required in the production application but will help us to detect memory leaks using Google Chrome Heap Profiler.

1. Add a named constructor to the each object in your program, which is extended from a standard Backbone object, such as Model or View. Inside this constructor, call a parent constructor.

    1. It could be much easier to detect memory leaks in Google Chrome Heap Profiler by finding object instances using their class names, which would only be possible if we defined such classes using named constructors.

    2. Following code shows the `InvoiceItemModel` object with the named constructor defined.

```
var InvoiceItemModel = Backbone.Model.extend({
  calculateAmount: function() {
    return this.get('price') * this.get('quantity');
  },

  constructor: function InvoiceItemModel() {
    InvoiceItemModel.__super__.constructor.apply(
      this, arguments
    );
  }
});
```

2. Make sure your application code is performed in a global scope. This will make it easier to find Backbone objects in Google Chrome Heap Profiler. Contents of your `main.js` file shouldn't be enclosed by any function. The next few lines of code should be removed from your `main.js` file.

```
(function($) {
  $(document).ready(function () {

  });
})(jQuery);
```

Inclusion of `main.js` into `index.html` should be performed in the `body` section as follows:

```
<body><script src="js/main.js"></script></body>
```

3. Modify `ControlsView` by adding a button which deletes `InvoiceItemsTableView` to demonstrate a memory leak. The following code explains how it works:

```
var ControlsView = Backbone.View.extend({
  render: function() {
    var html = '<br><input id="addModel" type="button" ' +
      'value="Add model" id><input id="removeModel" ' +
```

```
          'type="button" value="Remove model"><input ' +
          'id="removeTableView" type="button" ' +
          'value="Remove table view">';
     $(this.el).html(html);

     return this;
    },

    // Handle HTML events.
    events: {
      'click #addModel': 'addNewInvoiceItemModel',
      'click #removeModel': 'removeInvoiceItemModel',
      'click #removeTableView': 'removeInvoiceItemTableView',
    },

    //...

    // Remove a view button handler.
    removeInvoiceItemTableView: function() {
      this.options.invoiceItemTableView.remove();
    },
});

//...

invoiceItemTableView = new InvoiceItemTableView({
  collection: invoiceItemCollection
});

$('body').append(invoiceItemTableView.render().el);

$('body').append(new ControlsView({
  collection: invoiceItemCollection,
  invoiceItemTableView: invoiceItemTableView
}).render().el);
```

Our prepared application should look like the following image:

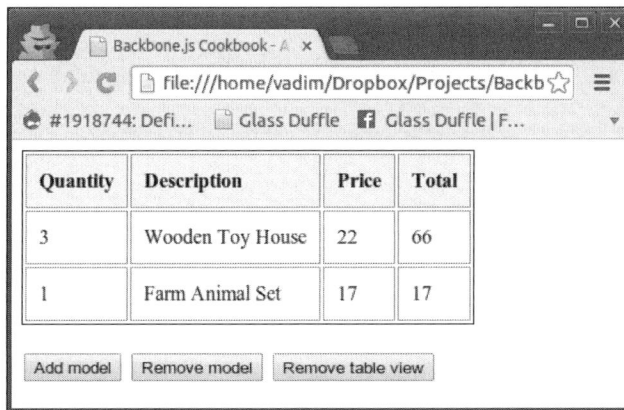

How to do it...

Perform the following steps to detect and to fix memory leaks in this application:

1. Open a web application in the **Chrome** browser.

2. Press the *F12* key to open **Chrome DevTool**.

3. Click on the **Profiles** tab and select the **Take Heap Snapshot** item.

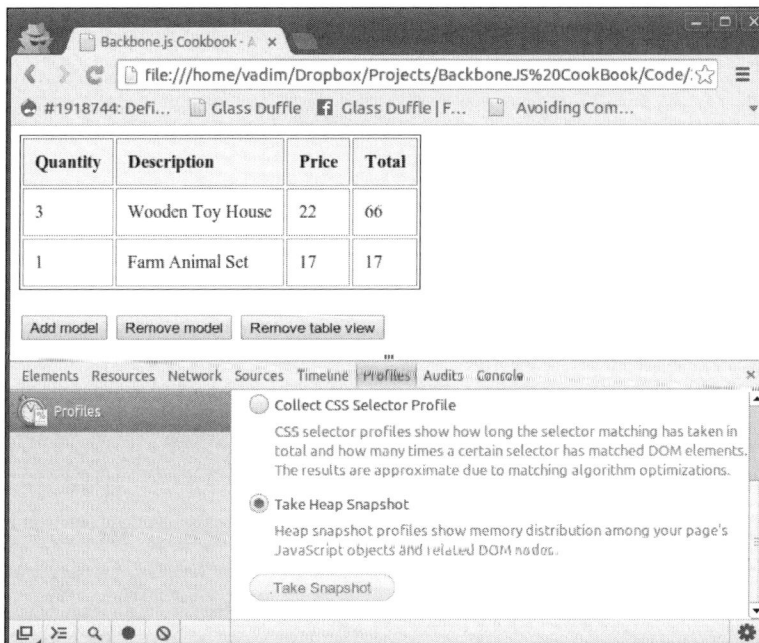

4. Click on the **Take Snapshot** button.

5. Enter `Invoice` in the **Class Filter** field.

6. You will see all the classes starting with an `Invoice` and an amount of their instances under the **Objects Count** column.

7. Click on the **Remove table view** button and take the heap snapshot once again to see a memory leak.

8. You will see that **Objects Count** was not decreased for any class but should have been.

9. Delete any references to objects from other objects when those references aren't required.

10. Delete references to the `InvoiceItemsTableView` instance after we called the `remove()` method.

```
var ControlsView = Backbone.View.extend({

  // ...

  removeInvoiceItemTableView: function() {
    this.options.invoiceItemTableView.remove();
    delete this.options.invoiceItemTableView;
  },
});
```

11. Delete all the child subviews when the parent view is removed.

12. In the following code, when the new sub-view is created, we assign its remove method as a handler to the clear event of the parent view. In the `remove()` method of the parent view, we trigger the clear event.

```
var InvoiceItemTableView = Backbone.View.extend({

    // ...

    append: function(model) {
        var view = new InvoiceItemView({ model: model });

        $(this.el).append(
            view.render().el
        );

        view.listenTo(this, 'clear', this.remove);
    },

    remove: function() {
        this.trigger('clear');

        return InvoiceItemTableView.__super__.remove.
        apply(
            this, arguments
        );
    }
});
```

13. Use `listenTo()` method instead of `on()` to bind callbacks to the events.

14. The `listenTo()` method keeps track of the bound events that unbinds them when the object is removed to make sure there is no any cyclic reference.

```
var InvoiceItemView = Backbone.View.extend({

    // ...

    initialize: function() {
        // Bind callback to destroy event of the model.
        this.listenTo(
            this.model, 'destroy', this.destroy, this
        );
    }
});
```

```
var InvoiceItemTableView = Backbone.View.extend({

    // ...

    initialize: function() {
        // Bind callback to add event of the collection.
        this.listenTo(
            this.collection, 'add', this.append, this
        );
    }
});
```

15. Reload the page, remove the table view, and then create a new heap snapshot to make sure no invoice views are leaked. We can still see some models are kept in the memory, but it happens because they are used by `ControlsView`.

See also

- ▶ The JavaScript Garbage Collector is described at the following location: `http://blogs.msdn.com/b/ericlippert/archive/2003/09/17/53038.aspx`

- ▶ Memory leaks' patterns in JavaScript are described at the following location: `http://www.ibm.com/developerworks/web/library/wa-memleak/`

Index

K

keyboard shortcuts
  handling, in view 136, 137

L

layouts
  assembling, LayoutManager used 163-166
length() method 68
length validator 51
LIFO (last in, first out) data structure 43
LinkedIn mobile 6
listenTo() method 117, 256
local storage
  working with 206, 207

M

many-to-many relationship
  implementing 89
map() method 76
maxLength validator 52
max validator 51
memento stack
  first state, restoring from 44
  working with 43, 44
memory leak
  about 250
  by closure 250
  detecting, Google Chrome Heap Profiler
    used 250-257
  in JavaScript, URL 258
minLength validator 51
min validator 51
mixins
  using, with Backbone objects 210, 211
mobile application
  developing, with jQuery Mobile 223-232
model
  about 29, 93
  adding, to collection 69
  adding, to collection at specific position 70
  advanced validation, using 49
  binding, to select list 134-136
  binding, to view 120-122

checking, for attribute 34
cloning 30
creating 30
default attribute values, setting 30, 31
default attribute values, setting with multiline
  expression 31, 32
existing models, adding 70
exporting, to JSON 89, 90
filtering, in collection 74
getting from collection, at specific index 67
getting from collection, by ID 69
HTML escaped attribute value, getting 34
multiple models, adding 70
nested attributes, working with 57, 58
removing, from collection 71
rendering, in view 99, 100
model attributes
  operating 33
  validating 35, 36
  validation errors, handling 36
  validation, triggering manually 37
model getters/setters
  overriding, Backbone.stickit used 132
model identifier
  operating 34, 35
model pair
  comparing 74
models and collections
  synchronizing, RESTful service used 185-187
models, of various types
  storing, in collection 83-85
model states
  managing 41
  operating 42, 43
model validation
  performing 155
mod_proxy_http module 246
mod_proxy module 246
mod_rewrite module 246
MongoDB Extended JSON
  about 212
  handling 188
MongoLab
  about 181
  creating 182-184
  URL 181, 212

used, for writing tests 216
working 218

R

rangeLength validator 52
range validator 51
records filtering
  performing 174
reduce() method 77
remove event 119
remove() method 71, 97, 255, 256
render() method 95, 102, 130, 143
Rendr 6
Representational State Transfer. *See* REST
require.config() function 243
required validator 50
Require.js file
  downloading 238
requirejs() function 239, 242
reset event 119
reset() method 71
resource URI 180
REST 180
REST API
  architecting 180
RESTful backend
  prototyping, with MongoLab 181
RESTful frontend
  building, with Backbone 190-201
RESTful service
  mocking up, with jQuery Mockjax 220-222
restore() method 42
R.js 244
route event 119
  params parameter 139
  route parameter 139
  router parameter 139
route:[name] event 119
router events
  handling 138, 139

S

save() method 36, 187
schema definition
  URL 152

search engines
  used, for ensuring compatibility 245-247
Seoserver
  about 245
  source repository 250
setElement() method 97, 100-102
set() method 33
setTemplates() method 161
setup() function 216, 219
shift() method 72
showDialog() method 228
Social Mobile Application 236
some() method 76
sort event 119
sort() method 73
specific HTML event
  listening to, Backbone.stickit used 133
stack
  about 72
  collection, working as 72
standard operators, No SQL operators
  $equal 80
  $exists 80
  $has 80
  $in 80
  $ne 80
  $nin 80
  about 79
  using 79, 80
start() function 25, 222
stickit() method 131
store() method 42
strictEqual() 218
subviews
  view, splitting into 103-106
switchPane() method 195, 196
sync event 119
sync() method 188

T

teardown() method 216, 221
template loader
  implementing 145, 146
templates
  splitting, into partials 144
  using, in view 142, 143

[PACKT] PUBLISHING open source*
community experience distilled

Thank you for buying
Backbone.js Cookbook

About Packt Publishing

Packt, pronounced 'packed', published its first book "*Mastering phpMyAdmin for Effective MySQL Management*" in April 2004 and subsequently continued to specialize in publishing highly focused books on specific technologies and solutions.

Our books and publications share the experiences of your fellow IT professionals in adapting and customizing today's systems, applications, and frameworks. Our solution based books give you the knowledge and power to customize the software and technologies you're using to get the job done. Packt books are more specific and less general than the IT books you have seen in the past. Our unique business model allows us to bring you more focused information, giving you more of what you need to know, and less of what you don't.

Packt is a modern, yet unique publishing company, which focuses on producing quality, cutting-edge books for communities of developers, administrators, and newbies alike. For more information, please visit our website: www.packtpub.com.

About Packt Open Source

In 2010, Packt launched two new brands, Packt Open Source and Packt Enterprise, in order to continue its focus on specialization. This book is part of the Packt Open Source brand, home to books published on software built around Open Source licences, and offering information to anybody from advanced developers to budding web designers. The Open Source brand also runs Packt's Open Source Royalty Scheme, by which Packt gives a royalty to each Open Source project about whose software a book is sold.

Writing for Packt

We welcome all inquiries from people who are interested in authoring. Book proposals should be sent to author@packtpub.com. If your book idea is still at an early stage and you would like to discuss it first before writing a formal book proposal, contact us; one of our commissioning editors will get in touch with you.

We're not just looking for published authors; if you have strong technical skills but no writing experience, our experienced editors can help you develop a writing career, or simply get some additional reward for your expertise.

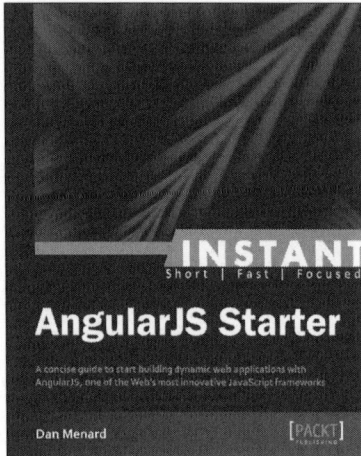

Instant AngularJS Starter

ISBN: 978-1-782166-76-4   Paperback: 66 pages

A concise guide to start building dynamic web applications with AngularJS, one of the Web's most innovative JavaScript frameworks

1. Learn something new in an Instant! A short, fast, focused guide delivering immediate results.

2. Take a broad look at the capabilities of AngularJS, with in-depth analysis of its key features

3. See how to build a structured MVC-style application that will scale gracefully in real-world applications

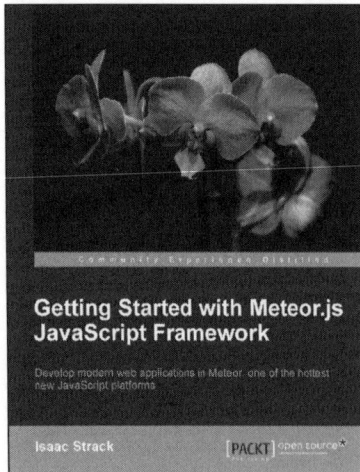

Getting Started with Meteor.js JavaScript Framework

ISBN: 978-1-782160-82-3   Paperback: 130 pages

Develop modern web applications in Meteor, one of the hottest new JavaScript platforms

1. Create dynamic, multi-user web applications completely in JavaScript

2. Use best practice design patterns including MVC, templates, and data synchronization

3. Create simple, effective user authentication including Facebook and Twitter integration

Please check **www.PacktPub.com** for information on our titles

Printed in Great Britain
by Amazon.co.uk, Ltd.,
Marston Gate.